QUEER POWER COUPLES

QUEER POWER COUPLES

ON
LOVE
AND
POSSIBILITY

WRITTEN BY HANNAH MURPHY WINTER &
PHOTOGRAPHED BY BILLIE WINTER

CHRONICLE BOOKS
SAN FRANCISCO

Library of Congress Cataloging-in-Publication Data
Names: Murphy Winter, Hannah, author. | Winter, Billie, photographer (expression)
Title: Queer power couples : on love and possibility / written by Hannah Murphy Winter & photographed by Billie Winter.
Description: San Francisco : Chronicle Books, [2024]
Identifiers: LCCN 2023034832 | ISBN 9781797214856 (hardcover)
Subjects: LCSH: Gay couples. | Lesbian couples.
Classification: LCC HQ76.34 .M87 2024 | DDC 306.84/8--dc23/eng/20230810
LC record available at https://lccn.loc.gov/2023034832

Manufactured in China.

Design by Evelyn Furuta.

10 9 8 7 6 5 4 3 2 1

Chronicle books and gifts are available at special quantity discounts to corporations, professional associations, literacy programs, and other organizations. For details and discount information, please contact our premiums department at corporatesales@chroniclebooks.com or at 1-800-759-0190.

Chronicle Books LLC
680 Second Street
San Francisco, California 94107
www.chroniclebooks.com

TO EVERYONE WHO
SHOWED US A MAP FOR
A QUEER FUTURE.

AND TO ANYBODY WHO
NEEDS ONE.

CONTENTS

INTRODUCTION

THE FIRST PERSON I ever recognized as queer was Spinelli from the cartoon *Recess*. (I'll give every millennial here a moment to google that and jog your memory.) And let's be clear: It was 1997, and no one ever *told* me she was queer. But this nine-year-old was relentlessly queer-coded: She went by her last name because she hated the name Ashley; she wore a leather jacket, black motorcycle boots, and a floppy yellow beanie; and for some reason, she had the gravelly voice of a forty-year-old Pall Mall smoker.

When the show came out, I was eight. I had no idea what the word *queer* meant—I'd only heard it as a synonym for *strange* in our house. And I'd never met anyone who was queer (that I knew of, at least). But I did know that Spinelli and I had something in common.

My wife, Billie, is nine years older than I am, so she missed the boat on *Recess*. (Her loss.) When we started this project, I asked her about the first person she recognized as queer. She remembered having a crush on Cheetara from *ThunderCats* when she was five years old, but she couldn't remember seeing *herself* in anyone. "Queerness felt like this secret that I had with myself," she told me. "But it was something that—in incredibly sharp clarity—I recognized in myself."

In high school, I'd finally learned what queerness was, but I still couldn't see my own. I joined my school's Gay Straight Alliance, but I joined as an "ally." And I wouldn't see a queer adult in real life until around that same time—my aunt's friend at a backyard barbecue. (I still remember fixating on her body language and what I can now describe as her *impeccable* lesbian jaw.) At that point, I was still so far from coming out to myself, let alone to the rest of the world: It would be years before I'd describe myself as queer, a decade before I'd get comfortable saying I was gay without dropping into hushed tones, and two before I'd start finding the words to describe my gender.

OPPOSITE PAGE:
Steven Norfleet and
Anthony Hemingway
in Los Angeles.

9

Coming out is rarely a fixed point in time, but Billie and I both say we came out when we were twenty-four. (When we told Molly Knox Ostertag, she slammed her hand on her desk: "That's the age! Twenty-four!" Apparently it was a trend among her queer friends.) It was a slow and awkward and fumbling process. We both grew up in liberal cities with liberal families—I was in Seattle; she was in New York—so we had some of the best chances of having access to LGBTQ representation. And yet we still had so few glimpses into what queerness could be and what queer adulthood could look like. One advocate would later describe it to me as "remaking yourself in the dark." (So much more on that later.)

Billie and I made this book together—me as the author, her as the photographer—and we spent three years interviewing queer power couples across generations, industries, and identities about queerness and visibility. In every conversation, we asked them the same question: Who was the first person you recognized as queer? They could be real or fictional, we said, out or closeted.

The question was usually met with excitement—it's a rare chance to talk about our queer origin stories—but it wasn't always easy to answer.

"I was raised in a really conservative home in Macon, Georgia," said musician Mackenzie Scott. "I didn't know any gay people. I didn't even know *of* any gay people at all, apart from Ellen and Rosie. And Elton John."

Most people did have a Spinelli, though. They found queerness in small moments or nuances: obliquely told stories about family friends, queer-coded characters like Miss Honey

from *Matilda,* or the tension of Victorian period dramas. One said he first saw himself in the backup dancers of Madonna's "Vogue" video; another, in Lamar from *Revenge of the Nerds.*

That recognition was always described as an "aha" moment, or an "I'm not alone" moment, or a "maybe there are more people out there like me" moment. But it was always framed a little bit like sifting for scraps, finding small pieces of our identities hidden away in otherwise unfamiliar people. And to find examples of couples—or of healthy queer love—was even more rare.

It brought us back to the question that started this project in the first place: Why hadn't a book about queer power couples been made yet? When we had started research for it in 2020, we found a few listicles—a new one comes out every year during Pride Month—and we found books celebrating queer love, queer celebrities, and even queer idols and their cats. But the notion of "queer power couples" didn't seem to have made it onto bookshelves.

A queer power couple, as we saw it, is at the intersection of three things: They're out, they're coupled, and they're able to influence mainstream culture. We realized that perhaps the reason this book hadn't been made yet was because, up until the last ten years, that intersection was pretty empty. And we had to recognize that the emptiness of that intersection was intentional: the result of decades of erasure and losing a generation of elders to the AIDS crisis, and not being able to see queer people grow up and age. And that was why everyone in this book talked about sifting for scraps—searching for allusions to queerness in popular culture to find proof that we're not alone.

THIS BOOK IS
A DOCUMENT OF
QUEER PEOPLE
TAKING UP
SPACE WITH BIG,
BEAUTIFUL
QUEER JOY.

But in 2020, that intersection had become busy enough that we were able to make whole lists of queer power couples. And so we wanted to ask the question: How does it feel to live at that intersection? We spent three years talking to some of the most interesting, influential LGBTQ people in their fields. And possibly most unique to this book, we explored an experience that's essentially new: being out and coupled and thriving in the public eye. We always say that coming out is a lifelong process, but what does it mean to also come out as a queer role model or mentor or power couple?

It's important to acknowledge, I think, that this collection of couples is virtually self-selected. We did make lists (so many lists) of people we would have loved to feature in this book, but unlike the listicles, everyone had to agree to be a part of this. They had to be excited by the premise and, more importantly, willing to spend time publicly diving into these questions of queer visibility, representation, love, and power.

We did find that some people in this book carry the responsibility of that representation a bit begrudgingly. But every single one of them remembered when they only had their Spinelli (or Miss Honey or Lamar), and because of that, they all took up the mantle of visibility consciously. Marilee Lindemann, a literary scholar at the University of Maryland, gives a speech to welcome students into her program every year, and every year she comes out to all nine hundred of them at once. "I know there are gay kids out there," she said when we spoke. "And I know that they come from places that aren't as safe and comfortable as the University of Maryland. And it's very important for me to let them know that I'm here, I'm queer, and I'm there for them."

These chapters represent so many queer experiences. But if you take away just one thing from this book, I hope it's queer joy. Outside of this project, I've been a journalist for more than a decade—Billie and I actually met at *Rolling Stone*—and I've consistently covered "LGBTQ issues." That means that, largely, I've written about queer pain: laws, legislatures, and entire administrations trying to erase us. This book is a document of queer people taking up space with big, beautiful queer joy.

That joy comes in so many forms, from the bombastic to the domestic. From a lavish, Black gay wedding in a castle overlooking the Santa Clara River Valley to a couple's daughter introducing them to her queer friend because she wanted him to see gay men just being "boring old dads."

"I've always loved that our relationship has been something that people could look up to," said musician Alan Wyffels. "Not only do people in our generation not have a lot of queer people in the public eye to look up to—but especially not relationships. We started to get a lot of feedback from people just being like, 'You guys give me so much hope that I'll be able to find something like you have someday.'"

As the intersection gets busier, we also have the chance to see just how many ways there are to be queer. Everyone in this book—and out of it—experiences queerness through the lens of other identities: female, immigrant, Black, Muslim, Christian, Southerner, scientist, parent. Which means chances are, that one queer scrap that you found in pop culture doesn't look or feel anything like you. "Growing up South Asian, on TV there was Mindy Kaling and Apu from *The Simpsons*. That *was* South Asian representation," said Fawzia Mirza, a Pakistani Canadian filmmaker. "And with Apu—well, he was animated—but also, am I supposed to *be* Apu? Marry Apu? How am I supposed to be a gay brown woman?"

"There's not a lot of maps still for a lot of queer experiences," said Mike Hadreas, Alan's partner and bandmate. For him, growing up in Seattle in the '90s, "it wasn't just about being queer. It was about being queer and weird. Or queer and dramatic. Or queer and creative. Because if there was any map, it was 'How to Assimilate.' Or 'How to Be Gay but Seem Straight.'" How could we know what our queer futures could look like when we'd never seen them?

Everyone in this book has played a role in making queer lives more visible. They've demonstrated that out, thriving queer people lead news organizations, chemistry labs, film sets, and nonprofits. They've celebrated queer storylines, bodies, and relationships in paint and music and film and television.

"Whether I knew I was doing it or not," Fawzia told us, "at some point, I made it my mission to be out and to love."

THIS BOOK WAS MADE IN THAT SPIRIT.

ON THE PHOTOGRAPHY

COMMITTING QUEERNESS TO FILM has always been a radical act.

When we first started research for this book, it was just after the fiftieth anniversary of the Stonewall Riots. At the time, we worked right across the street from the central branch of the New York Public Library, and they had just put up a sprawling exhibit of queer photography from the Stonewall era. It came from the archives of Kay Tobin Lehusen and Diana Davies, and it was a record of undeniable queer love in small, ordinary gestures: a face popping out of the shower curtain, the way someone plays with their partner's hair when they're sitting on a couch, or how they absentmindedly reach for their hand in a crowd. Every image was an act of protest.

We knew that any effort to document queer love was part of a long, radical history, and we were curious what the photographers of that era would have to say about queer visibility today. Many of them had already passed—I found Lehusen's obituary days after we started this project, and Alvin Baltrop's estate was only able to point us to a few old news clippings. But Joan E. Biren—known to most everyone as JEB—was just coming off the press whirlwind from the reissue of her 1979 collection, *Eye to Eye: Portraits of Lesbians* ("the first openly lesbian photography book of lesbians, by a lesbian, to be published in the US," as she describes it). She told us she wasn't able to do an interview, but she could send us her thoughts on queer visibility. She wrote:

> Being seen as who you are is fundamental to establishing a shared identity and building community. Visibility for queer folx is what makes a movement possible. Organizing cannot be done from inside the closet. But we must understand that visibility can be more or less dangerous depending on one's position of power and privilege in society.

OPPOSITE PAGE:
Jenna Gribbon and Mackenzie Scott, taken by Jenna.

She saw something that's easy to overlook when you're talking about queer power couples—that visibility is a privilege that everyone experiences differently.

For their photo shoots, we asked the couples to choose how they wanted to be visible by selecting a location that was part of the world they'd built together. Many of them chose their homes, but many didn't: We met in hotels, studios, campsites—anywhere that felt like *theirs*. The photography is a document of queer intimacy and a claiming of queer space.

Every couple in this book was generous with their time, energy, and hearts, and that made it possible to genuinely capture that intimacy. Throughout the project, we wanted to let people tell their stories in their own voices, wherever we could. So, in the same way that the chapters are largely written in their own voices, at the end of each photo shoot Billie literally put the camera in the subjects' hands—a point-and-shoot loaded with black-and-white film—to photograph one another. As Billie says, they'll never look at her the way they look at each other.

Sean and Terry Torrington in Brooklyn.

WE KNEW THAT ANY
EFFORT TO DOCUMENT
QUEER LOVE WAS PART
OF A LONG, RADICAL
HISTORY.

REMAKING YOURSELF IN THE DARK

OVER THE LAST THREE YEARS, I asked almost everyone we interviewed what they thought of Mike Hadreas's metaphor: that we don't have enough "maps" for what queer lives can look like.

To my delight, everyone seemed to have their own metaphor—like we'd all invented our own language before we were able to talk to one another. Heron Greenesmith, an LGBTQ policy expert, called it "remaking yourself in the dark." They're bisexual, trans, and agender—a sort of perfect storm of erasure, even in the queer community. When you're coming out, they said, "You open the door, and instead of a bunch of people saying, 'Surprise! We're so glad you're here!' the room is just pitch-black."

OPPOSITE PAGE:
Samantha Beaird and Aisha Ibrahim in Redmond, WA.

Instead of "maps," then, their metaphor is torches—lighting a path in the dark. "I have a yearning to be seen," they said. "To have people hold up torches and say, 'Look, your shadow looks like mine.'"

All of the interviews in this book span questions of queerness and visibility, but the chapters in this section offer a particular insight to the beginning of that journey: when you're remaking yourself in the dark. Mike talks about being a teenager in the '90s and looking for maps for how to be queer and *not* assimilate; ND Stevenson describes growing up in an Evangelical home and having to let go of the only possible future he'd ever imagined—as a soccer mom, married to a man in a Christian home.

Queer kids typically aren't born into queer families. Our torches and our maps are almost never found at home. So having queer love and queer joy—queer life—out in public is quite literally a matter of survival.

ND Stevenson and Molly Knox Ostertag at Figueroa Mountain in California.

Dr. Ilan Meyers is a researcher at UCLA's Williams Institute, a public policy think tank that focuses on sexual orientation and gender identity. He told me about a study from Chicago in the '90s that found that "young gay people, compared to straight people, were less likely to even project their life into older ages"—that they couldn't imagine what it would look like to live a full life as a queer person.

"There's an old psychological concept called 'possible self,'" Dr. Meyers said. "When you're young, you imagine your future. And the kinds of things that you imagine are the things that you can strive for." Our imaginations are made up of what we can see around us—in our lives, on TV, and in the news. Kids who identify as straight often have countless examples in the media for what their romantic, sexual, and professional futures could look like. "Not having the images of LGBTQ success—and of successful couples, specifically—is very relevant to that notion of how people can envision a happy life."

In 2021, the year we started interviewing couples, pop culture and entertainment were embracing queer storylines and storytellers in a way that we'd never seen—from queer teens on *Sex Education*, *Euphoria*, and *Generation*, to Emily Dickinson in the very queer historical drama *Dickinson*. That season, GLAAD calculated that 12 percent of all characters on prime-time TV were queer. But 2021 also saw the most anti-LGBTQ legislation introduced into state legislatures in history. Then 2022 beat that record. Then 2023 broke it again.

Whether you call them "maps" or "torches" or "possible selves," Dr. Meyers thinks these images can be a potent antidote to the political narratives that queer kids are exposed to. During the same-sex marriage debate, studies found that even though the policy ultimately awarded LGBTQ people more rights, "just the way that our lives were debated in that fashion" did real psychological harm, he says. It's important for kids to "have the alternative view."

"A happy gay couple," he says, "is, in the context of history, a very revolutionary idea."

MIKE HADREAS

(HE/HIM)
FOUNDER OF
PERFUME GENIUS

ALAN WYFFELS

(HE/HIM)
FOUNDING MEMBER
OF PERFUME GENIUS

WHEN I ASK MIKE HADREAS if he remembers the first person he recognized as queer, he answers slowly. He and Alan are sitting at their dining room table in their house in Los Angeles. They are both angled gently toward each other: Alan seems to broaden his shoulders as he listens; Mike pulls his knees into his chest.

"The only thing I can think of is—I must've been six or five—and there was a TV movie about a gay man, and Julie Andrews was his mom," he says. "And all I remember is he's dying of AIDS, and she was tending to him." He is talking about the 1991 made-for-TV drama *Our Sons*. It follows the struggles of two homophobic moms overcoming their homophobia while one son dies of complications from AIDS. Reviewers at the time graciously said the film "means well."

"For some reason, I was watching with my mom, and I remember going to bed that night thinking that was going to be me," Mike says. "Maybe it's because I saw a representation of how bad I felt—how outsider-y and like I had done something really wrong all the time."

He started imagining the two possible futures he saw for himself, literally, on the wall in his bedroom. He would imagine a wheel on the wall: one side said "gay"; the other, "not gay." And he would spin it in his mind over and over again. "I wouldn't fall asleep until it would land on 'not gay,'" he says while he mimes spinning the wheel. "This is all my brain—I was making it happen—but it would always land on 'gay.'"

"It did help me get over it, though," he tells me. "I only did that until I was like ten. And then I was like, 'Okay, I'm done. I'm gay. It's over.' Doing it that early, I think it helped me be so exhausted from it that I just had to come out to myself—and then everybody else—pretty early."

When I turn to Alan, he tosses his hand up.

ALAN: I never really came out. I don't have a coming-out story. I was such a freaky little troubled teen that my sexuality—people weren't worried that much about it. They were more worried about me not ODing or getting arrested. My dad walked in on me hooking up with one of my friends, and he found a bunch of *Playgirl* magazines in my closet. And I knew that he knew and we just didn't talk about it.

And then one day I just brought a guy home and was like, "Hey, this is my boyfriend," and they were just like, "Okay, cool." But I never had a moment where I sat them down like on TV shows and stuff like that.

What I remember, though: When I was like nine or ten, my dad had married his second wife, who was an alcoholic—a really toxic, damaged person. And we were in the pool in our backyard. And she was like, "You know, your dad is terrified that you're going to grow up to be gay." And I knew what being gay was at that time, but honestly, at that point, hadn't really thought a lot about it. I just remember being mortified by that. And I think that probably affected my willingness to talk about it with my family.

It's weird growing up and having people tell you you're gay before you even really fully understand what that is. It made me wonder—when I was first coming to terms with being gay—if I was just sort of a self-fulfilling prophecy. All these people were telling me that I was, so was I just like, "I guess I'll be that."

"I obviously don't feel that way now," says Alan.

Today, Mike is best known by his stage name, Perfume Genius; but maybe a bit paradoxically, he and Alan together are *also* Perfume Genius—Alan is the only other original member of the band. And together, for the last decade, they've recorded, toured, and traveled the world from a stance that is inescapably and unapologetically queer.

Perfume Genius was born when Mike's whole life was in transition. It was 2010, and he'd just left New York, moved back in with his mom, and was trying to get sober. He reached out to someone who

he knew was already sober ("Which was baffling to me," he says), and that friend started taking him to some ("very queer") meetings with some of his other sober buddies, including his friend Alan.

"All three of us started just banding together," says Mike. "It was very teenager-like. We were all together every day." It was a moment that felt full of possibility. "When you're getting sober, it's a tough time for everybody. But it was also really fun and exploratory. It's almost like you can smell again; you can see again. It's like things come back, and you feel like a little kid."

ALAN: I remember the day that I met Mike for the first time. I'd been sober for like a year, and there was this group of sober people that would go out and dance and stuff. This was my first time doing that, and Mike was there at this club. I remember he was sitting down against the wall, and I was just staring at him. I have a bit of a staring problem as it is, but I don't even think I realized how intensely I was staring at him. But it was enough that he was kind of like, "Okay, dude, what's going on?"

MIKE: Because he doesn't break eye contact either. If you catch him, he just stays, you know what I mean? But I can be very shy, and I was feeling a little shy.

ALAN: It was funny. I know this sounds corny or maybe hard to believe, but it's happened to me a few times where I've met people and just instantly known that they were going to have some big impact on my life. And I had that with Mike. I just knew in that moment— there's something here.

Around that same time, Mike had started uploading music to MySpace under the name Perfume Genius—ambient explorations of queerness and recovery. One day, he got a call from Matador Records. "It was a freak internet thing," says Alan. "He literally got a record deal from MySpace." The problem, though, was that Mike had never performed before. The solution? Alan.

ALAN: He came to me and he's like, "I have to play some shows. And I've never done that before. I know you're a musician. Will you help me figure out how to do that?"

Alan had studied music in college, and Mike knew he was a talented pianist.

ALAN: I was like, "Sure." I thought we were gonna play some open mics or something. And then he's like, "Yeah, our first shows are in Seattle, New York, Paris, and London." I was like, "What."

MIKE: And I had never sung in front of anybody. He's the first person I ever even sang in front of, when we were practicing. And I mean, I was in love with him. I'm sure that factored into me asking him to play. But also, he went to school for music—he was technical and trained in a way that I wasn't. I didn't really know what I was doing. And I knew that he was very capable musically.

ALAN: I always thought Mike asked me to play with him as a way to weasel his way in.

MIKE: Maybe! I mean, I was very witchy about Alan. A lot of my energy was taken up with trying to get Alan. I was pulling out all the stops without actually saying anything. I was just pointing all of my energy toward him.

ALAN: But for the first six months, we were just friends. I had a massive crush on Mike, but I didn't really think it was reciprocal. Also, when you're in early recovery, they recommend that you don't get involved in relationships because a lot of people just replace drugs or alcohol with people, you know? And so I didn't want to be like this lecherous creeper swooping in to try to date Mike.

And he felt the same way—he was having these feelings but didn't think that I was having the feelings. So this went on for six months, and we were just practicing together and hanging out all the time but just both had this simmering obsession with the other person. And then one day it all came out and we moved in together a week later.

"We were together twenty-four seven for like ten years after that," Alan says. Those ten years included six albums and as many tours. I asked them what it meant for their relationship, to come together on their first world tour and, essentially, onstage.

MIKE: It's hard to articulate. Because I was the happiest I've ever been. I felt completely freaked out. It was really overwhelming. But I just felt like I was where I was supposed to be. I was with who I'm supposed to be with. I was doing what I'm supposed to be doing. It was just good. And it was real and wholesome. And I don't know—it was really a beautiful time.

ALAN: Those tours that we did—when it was just the two of us—it was really special. The music was so deeply personal and people were coming up after the shows just bawling their eyes out and so many people just relating so intensely—having these really visible reactions to the shows. It was really intense. There was something about the intimacy of those first shows that was really amazing.

MIKE: We wore the same thing offstage as we did onstage, you know what I mean? There's no real separation. I felt like we just kind of just walked onstage, lived in front of people for a little bit, and walked offstage. That's how it felt. And that's just what I thought you're supposed to do. It was very wild.

We saw them perform a few months before we meet them in person. Their touring band was larger than in the original days, but the heart of Perfume Genius was still Mike and Alan. Wrapped in fog under blue light, Mike was magnetically weird—kinetic, ethereal, swishy. Alan was *just* in the penumbra—sculpted and sturdy behind the keyboard. He still stared at Mike. Mike didn't seem to mind.

At their house, though, when they open their front door, the spotlight is immediately stolen by the third member of their family: a graying Chihuahua named Wanda whose list of people she likes begins and ends with them. Mike and Alan are, at their core, cozy people. Mike is reclining on a couch that looks like it was chosen specifically because the thigh-to-cushion ratio makes it difficult to get out of. When they're not on tour, that's where they spend most of their time, they say: Mike, Alan, and Wanda and a marathon of *The Comeback*. "We're such nesters," Alan says. But because they're "always moving"—from Seattle to Tacoma to Los Angeles in the last few years alone—they don't feel attached to any one house that they've lived in. Instead, "the way we make a home *is* the home."

Knowing that—and the fact that their relationship basically exists because of their music—I expected Perfume Genius to have a huge presence in their home. But when I ask where Mike writes, he points to "the place over there that looks like a storage room." Down a few stairs from the living room, there's an exercise machine, a pile of discarded clothes, and a table with a keyboard.

ALAN: Mike does all the writing—at least the beginning parts of it—on his own. And it has always been very dramatic: He has to lock himself away and not leave the house for a month to get in the zone to do that. And then I come in and help him flesh things out later on in the process. But Mike, I think, is a very isolated, creative person. And I think collaboration—it's just challenging for you.

MIKE: Like true collaborators. I can be hands off and let people do whatever. But making stuff together from scratch is hard. I don't know how to do it.

ALAN: I went to Mexico for a week, and he wrote this last record. An entire record. And it makes me think, do I need to get my own apartment? Would it be more productive?

MIKE: I think it's a safety thing. I think writing is when I finally let it all come out. It removes all the noise around everything. But when I first start making something, I don't want to hear anything negative; I can't stand it. Because this is a time where I have to really hype myself up. I get kind of manic, build myself up, so can I start drawing stuff out.

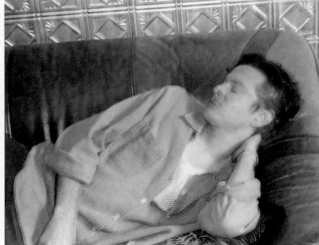

Alan, photographed by Mike.

Mike, photographed by Alan.

That's only the first stage, though. Alan comes from a classical background—he's studied music, learned theory, and embraced the value of rehearsal. "I hate rehearsal," says Mike. "I hate practicing. Anything that feels like work, I hate it. It feels like it's removing me from the magic of exploring and being and making." It makes Alan somewhat of a mystery to him. "Alan gets to that magic place by rehearsal and working and critical thinking. I think that's really cool and wild." And it might be those opposing approaches that make Perfume Genius's music so exciting.

ALAN: What inspires me about Mike is his fearlessness as an artist. Mike never thought he was going to be a musician. It kind of just happened. And the fact that he has been able to turn it into a career and all the scary things that he's had to do . . . Even just the first show we played together, I was not certain he was gonna come out onstage. He was so petrified. I was like, "This might not happen, and we're about to find out." And you know, he came out. There've been so many situations where I've been so codependently freaking out for him where he's just, like, totally cool, shows up, and is able to just put himself out there in this really vulnerable way. And I just don't know where that comes from.

Mike may not have expected to be musician, but he still spent his childhood looking up to them. "Mike always said that he wanted to be an artist that he wished he would have had as a teen," Alan says. Growing up in Seattle, Mike was always looking for queer idols onstage.

MIKE: I think I've seen Sleater-Kinney thirteen times. And it was aspirational—I was like thirteen, and I was seeing all these queer people in a room and seeing queer people onstage singing about being queer and being all together and having fun too. Rufus Wainwright—anybody that was out, who was making good work, it gave me a lot of hope. I connected to it as like, "Oh, I can feel the way I do. I can be this way. And there's things that can happen and stuff to be made and other people that can feel the same way." It wasn't just about being queer. It was about being queer and weird. Or queer and dramatic. Or queer and creative.

Because if there was any map, it was "How to Assimilate." Or "How to Be Gay but Seem Straight." And I knew from very early on that was not going to be my story.

ALAN: I didn't feel like I was even looking for that really until much later. When I was in my twenties, I moved into this house with twelve queer people and the guy I was dating at that time, but before that, I wasn't really searching for queer community or even looking for queer idols. All my idols were women.

MIKE: That's always the thing!

ALAN: I think it's interesting to see even now. I feel like you see a lot of people talking about, like, "Why do queer people not lift up other queer people in the industry?" And most gay men, they just listen to women. They don't listen to other queer men. Gay culture is very much just, like, Lady Gaga and Ariana Grande and pop divas.

Especially in the early '90s, though, when they were both growing up, comparing queer artists and pop divas was a distinction without a difference. Queer culture—especially Black queer culture—was being synthesized and released as hetero, white, radio-ready pop. Even at ten years old, Alan clocked it.

ALAN: I remember the first time I saw Madonna's "Vogue" video—seeing all the men in that video, all these queer men. The way they were moving—it was very clear to me. I remember I was very young, and I was like, "I don't know what exactly is going on there, but I want to know what's happening there." And I'm pretty sure that's the first time I saw any sort of queerness on television. That, to me, was the moment I was like, "What is that? I want that."

He has it now. And he and Mike get to represent another version of queerness in the public eye. Their security with each other, and with their queerness, is one of the things that's made Perfume Genius stand out over the years. In 2017—two years after the Supreme Court decision on gay marriage—a reviewer for NPR noted that, even then, "Queer music has been largely about the struggle of finding that sort of security. Hadreas's music represents a new challenge, in which two men must now map out how to live within that security."

The closing track on their 2017 album, *No Shape*, is titled "Alan." Mike sings:

Did you notice we sleep through the night

Did you notice, babe, everything's all right

You need me, rest easy

I'm here, how weird

And years later, that's still true.

MIKE: Neither of us have anything to reference it against. In the beginning, it was just me and Alan on tour. We were the only musicians, so it was just me and him at every show for years. And we played one of the songs as a duet together—we're both on the same piano and singing. And I wasn't thinking about what kind of information, specifically, that made. But also, we were in love, and the music is just queer by nature. Because I am and we are.

Over the years, it became more deliberate, like all those things. I knew people were coming to the shows—and eventually I could look at them and I wasn't too nervous. It became more intentional. And I valued and loved what our relationship and the kind of things I write about could mean to other people.

ALAN: I've always loved that our relationship has been something that people could look up to, because I think not only do people in our generation not have a lot of queer people in the public eye—but especially not relationships. We started to get a lot of feedback from people just being like, "You guys give me so much hope that I'll be able to find something like you have someday."

I think that kids growing up now, with all the apps—I think it's, like, very "hookup culture." And I think a lot of people just think that that's what being queer is. They don't see a lot of long-term relationships. And I think that being able to be an example that, "Yeah, actually, you can be queer and be in a functional long-term relationship if you want that," [is important].

MIKE: Yeah. Because there's not a lot of maps still for a lot of queer experiences. Which is one of the most beautiful things about it—that you kind of get to make it up, make your own frameworks. But it also is comforting to see where you *could* go.

MOLLY KNOX OSTERTAG

(SHE/HER)
COMIC ARTIST
AND TV WRITER

___

ND STEVENSON

(HE/HIM)
COMIC ARTIST
AND SHOWRUNNER

___

"UM, HOW DETAILED DO YOU WANT TO GO?" ND asks Molly.

They're telling their "how they met" story—and like most couples who've been together for a while, it's well choreographed.

"It's a really good story," Molly says.

Molly and ND had both been up-and-coming comic artists—phrases like *best and brightest* and *artists to watch* were getting thrown around a lot. They had popped up on each other's radar when they were both in art school, and they ended up on the same "Web Comics You Should Be Reading" list.

MOLLY: I remember my friend showing your Tumblr to me, back in the day. And he was like, "Oh, you guys look really similar"—white girl, little pixie that people presumed was queer, but, like, *we* didn't know that we were queer. And I remember being like, "Oh, ND makes, like, fan art. I'm better than that."

ND: Our enemies-to-lovers arc.

They went to all the same comic conventions and events, so they were always in each other's periphery. They barely knew each other, really, but "ND would make these incredibly intimate and vulnerable comics," Molly tells me. "And I would just see them and be like, 'Oh, my God, I feel very connected to this person.' And so that was very, very intense."

"I was still a little like, 'Who's this bitch?'" ND says. "But I felt this draw right away."

In 2015, they had both been headed to the Toronto Comic Arts Festival. And this is the part of the story where they aren't sure how detailed to get.

MOLLY: I was driving from New York, a nine-hour drive. This car was packed with indie comics' best and brightest, and we got in a crazy car accident. Everyone was okay, but our tire blew and we spun off the road and flipped several times. It was really scary.

But we got there eventually. We left the car at a junkyard, rented a car, and continued driving to TCAF. And so I was tweeting, "Oh, my gosh, this happened to me."

ND: And I saw the tweet. And I had this reaction that, "Oh, my god, Molly almost died." And this emotion that was just like, I can't—I like—I have to like—

MOLLY: I was also having emotions.

Today, ND and Molly are both known—and celebrated—for writing, creating, and illustrating deeply, beautifully queer stories. ND broke onto the scene with *Lumberjanes* and *Nimona*, a comic about a gender-fluid shape-shifter (which was adapted into an animated movie in 2023), and he's the creator and showrunner of Netflix's *She-Ra and the Princesses of Power*, a reboot of the 1985 cartoon transformed into a queer, pastel fantasia. Molly is the *New York Times* bestselling author of *The Witch Boy* (which Netflix is turning into an animated feature with a score by Haim) and the coming-out selkie tale *The Girl from the Sea*. She's also a writer on Disney's Peabody Award–winning show *The Owl House*. (If you watch only one of her episodes, might I recommend the queer history-making "Enchanting Grom Fright.")

But at TCAF in 2015, neither of them was out, and ND was years away from thinking about his trans-ness or gender identity.

ND: As soon as she got there, I just was like, "All right, I'm buying your drink. I'm taking care of you this week. Come with me." And so everyone came back to my hotel room, and we hung out into the wee hours and people started leaving a little bit at a time. And it was what, like two, three in the morning?

MOLLY: It was very early.

And Molly's Airbnb was a long walk away. "And I accidentally rented the presidential suite without realizing it, so I had this enormous double king bed," ND says. So Molly stayed the night "and somehow, in this giant bed, ended up very much on my side. And we ended up cuddling through the night."

ND: I slept very little. I don't even know if I woke up. I was just frozen in place all night. And in the morning I went and I jumped in the shower, and then avoided you for the rest of the convention. Because I was freaking out. And then eventually, I was just like, "Okay, something's happening here. And I don't know how real it is."

They lived on opposite coasts, and in some ways, it was easier to have big queer feelings when the object of those feelings was on the opposite side of the country. Part of the challenge was trying to reimagine how their communities would perceive them.

MOLLY: I think I was sort of starting to come out to people as bisexual, because I knew that was a part of me, and I wanted them to know.
       On the face of it, I was not visibly queer. I was definitely trying to hold both of those things—the past and also what I wanted my future to be.

ND: The first time you talked on Twitter about being bi, you did a drawing for Bisexual Visibility Day. And on the one hand, I was like, "Hell yeah. Molly's bi. I have a shot."

And on the other hand, the drawing she had done was, like, two girls cuddling in a bed. And one of them kind of looked like me. And I was like, "What does it mean?!"

"I couldn't get her out of my head," he wrote years later in an illustrated coming-out story. "I posted little drawings that, secretly, were just for her—and she responded with drawings that seemed like they were just for me."

MOLLY: It was cool to just fall in love with you before I really knew you, through your work. You would make these achingly vulnerable things, and all I wanted was to be with you. (I think that's a line I got from *Love Actually*.)

The illustrations were part love letter and part code. But they were also a way to say the things they couldn't say out loud yet. "It's kind of scary to use a word before you're ready," Molly says. "The first time I said *lesbian* I was playing a character in a D&D campaign. I was like, 'I'm just gonna play a lesbian just to see what it's like.'"

It took about a year for them to finally become a couple, but when they did, it stuck. When we met in 2021, they'd been married for two years. Their wedding was at Big Bear Lake. There were bonfires. And swords.

They don't have to look for codes in each other's illustrations anymore, but their stories clearly permeate their home (lovingly called "Wife City" and shared with their dog, Winston, and their two cats, Fig and Toast). And it's been that way since day one.

"When we first got together," ND says, "I was in the process of pitching *She-Ra*." Spoiler alert in the next paragraph, if anyone hasn't seen the show yet. (Go watch it.)

ND: I remember this one day where I was like, I need a big twist for the series. And Molly, without even looking up, just goes, "The planet's a weapon." And I was like, "Oh, that's brilliant!" Molly's voice as a storyteller and point of view and narratives—that was a big part of what I admired so much about her.

These stories are not just our job. They're also how we see the world. Being able to talk story with Molly and see the world through her eyes—and I think vice versa as well—it's just such a big part of both of us.

MOLLY: [Our relationship] honestly has felt like an ongoing master class in storytelling.

I started out by drawing other people's stories. And I think it was only when we were really dating that you were like, "Hey, you should push to do your own." And I was very insecure about it. I don't share my in-progress work quite as much. So usually, when I do, I get really nervous that ND's gonna read it and then come out and be like, "I hate it. We're divorcing." And you always like it.

ND: Yeah, I come out of the office crying.

Their home is an incubator for so many of their ideas, and that means that they both touch each other's work, even if they have nothing to do with it.

ND: I always thought that for stories to be interesting, the characters couldn't get what they wanted. They had to be put through the ringer, and the payoff had to be at the very end. And it had to be bittersweet. I just assumed that's what made a compelling narrative, especially when it came to romance. And Molly has really changed my mind about that. Molly's stories are always focused on the *existence* of characters. It's creating drama out of the connections between people and their own inner life.

MOLLY: I want to see stories and to make stories where people are just together. I want to see their relationships evolve. I want to see them evolve individually and together. And I don't want to wait till the end.

ND: She completely changed my mind about what tension can be in storytelling because, of course, her stories still have that tension; they still have that longing and the friction and the drama and all of it. She really took me out of this little bit of a box that I had in my own thinking of what friction can look like.

She just has this point of view that not a lot of people have—that characters can be soft, these arcs can be quiet and they can be relatable, and they can look like the relationships we have in real life.

They seem to have built a life that is always open to inspiration, wherever it might come from. "I've gotten Molly way too into reality TV," ND says. *Ink Master* is a household favorite. "Because I find it so interesting. It's such an interesting character study. Reality TV is trash a lot of the time, but for me it's also this constant conflict between who each person is trying to be versus who they really are."

I ask them, if even reality TV can become work, how do they ever stop working?

"We go camping," Molly says. "We have to leave our house." And so when we ask where they might like to do their photo shoot for this book—a place that represents the worlds that they've built together—a campsite is their first thought.

We meet them on the top of a winding mountain road with no guard rails and views that, on a clear day, span the full twenty miles to the ocean.

When we arrive at the campsite, I remember that in addition to her bestselling books, Molly is also a well-known *Lord of the Rings* fanfic writer. Her stories center around hobbits—particularly the relationship between Frodo and Sam. And at the campsite, it suddenly makes sense. Molly *is* a hobbit. Half of her camping gear is pots and pans. When she arrives, she sets up a "gear line" in a tree to hold all her food containers and utensils. She cooks us a multicourse meal, all over the fire.

ND and Molly do seem to be able to take a break—at least at the top of a mountain with no reception. Their dog, Winston, snuffles around in the dust while they take in views, set up camp, and explore the trails around the campsite. They chat kindly with a neighboring camper who unilaterally named himself the mayor of the site. And wherever they are, their pinkies seem to absentmindedly find each other and hook together.

But stories are still clearly everywhere for them. In the food they make, the worlds they build, and the tales they tell around the fire (ND told one that spooked us so much, we ditched our tent and slept in the car that night).

ND: I think we would be telling stories whether or not we actually had jobs as storytellers. It's just a part of us. Work is really difficult. And when I was in the depths of *She-Ra*, every single thing was about *She-Ra*. I go see a movie and I'm like, "Oh, what's that organ they're using in the soundtrack? I'm gonna give that to our composer." That can mean a complete demolition of boundaries between work and home life.

But you also have to have experiences. You have to grow as a person before you can tell stories that are really truthful. And so we try to have hobbies and have friendships that aren't just about working in animation or in comics or in storytelling.

MOLLY: We don't have the same working style—we actually work really differently. But we both understand "I'm on deadline." Or "I have to work really hard." Or "My brain is exhausted, and I need to just watch the dumbest shit tonight because I can't watch something smart." Or "I'm not engaged in life right now because I'm really caught up in work."

We get it. We have that common language that I think is really special, because I think if either of us had a more normal job, it would be hard to explain: Sometimes the inspiration is running and I have to be working right now. I know it's not going to come back for a while. So I need to take advantage.

In June 2022, a few weeks after our camping trip, ND posted a comic on social media. When we first met ND and Molly the year before, ND was beginning to talk about his gender journey. He was still using all personal pronouns and was loosely going by "ND," personally and professionally.

In the comic, a cartoon ND waves: "My name is ND! And my pronouns are he/him! . . . but I am not (entirely) a boy." He says he chose a "male" name and "male" pronouns "because this is how I want to interact with a world that demands we choose one of two; but I am not one of two." He kept his middle name, Diana, as "a way of paying tribute to this other side of me. I may keep it hidden and close to my heart, but I am not ashamed of it. It is mine and no one else's." Professionally, he goes by ND—Nate Diana—honoring both parts of him.

"I wanted to wait until I was absolutely sure of everything," he wrote, "which I still am not, if I'm being honest. There's never been some magic compass inside telling me which way to go, just little things that add up over time."

When we talk, I ask them what it's been like to come out, repeatedly, in the public eye. They were already well known when they met. Molly is quick to say that ND was the famous one, but people did—and still do—pay close attention to them, their work, and their relationship, for better and for worse.

ND: It's been kind of a push and pull. I've been going through a journey with gender in the last year and a half, and I think in some ways, I'm less likely to claim an identity really strongly than Molly is. I feel like you claim certain words, sometimes almost in defiance of what people expect from those words.

And for me, I don't. It's very hard for me to keep my interior relationship with myself a secret. I do tend to overshare in general, but I'm also more likely to be like, "I'm not putting a label on it yet." I'm leaving myself an open door to get out if I need to. And I've come to realize it's just part of the process for me. You can't force a flower to open any faster than it is. And I am a special flower!

But I think in a lot of ways, we have different styles of engaging with our own relationship with ourselves. The courage and the way that Molly proclaims herself is always very inspiring to me.

What words has Molly claimed in defiance?

MOLLY: I love *lesbian*. I love the word *woman* for myself. It's funny, I feel like in our friend group, every single person has come out as trans in the last year, if they were not already. And I'm kind of just hanging out. But there's something about putting my pin in—I use that phrase a lot—putting your pin in something and being like, "This is what I am."

It's a complicated word—people love to try to make it smaller than it is. People love to be very transphobic about it: "Oh, you can't have a relationship with a trans man and call yourself a lesbian." There's a lot of people who really love to winnow down that word. For me, it feels very expansive and very big.

ND: And being cis—there's so much gender exploration that comes with that as well—of being like, "My definition of *woman* for myself is not founded on anyone else's."

MOLLY: And having both trans women, who maybe realize womanhood is something to love and fight for, and then also having trans men and trans masculine people in my life, I'm realizing I am not obligated to be a woman if I do not want to be. And so arriving at that and finding that really deep, deep love of my gender and approaching it from the perspective of trans people in my life has been really cool.

I think people should think a lot about their gender. Because even if you just find out that you are your assigned gender, it still is like, "This is not a destiny that was foisted on me. This is something I'm choosing every day." If you're gonna be a gender, it's worth loving what that is and feeling good in it.

ND: And if you're *not* gonna be a gender, it's also worth loving! Your gender or lack thereof.

MOLLY: The more I've explored it, and really learned so much about the trans experience, it gives me new language to love myself in a really cool way.

In ND's announcement, he also wrote about the physical changes in his transition. "I love that our biology is malleable, that our bodies are ours to shape," he wrote. "It's not always easy (no body is easy), but

I never knew it was possible to feel this kind of joy and freedom in my form before, like I'm feeling grass beneath my feet for the very first time."

Both Molly and ND have the vocabulary of people who've had to find ways to convey their experience, over and over again, to the people around them, and to themselves. For ND, that started in the conservative Evangelical community that he grew up in in South Carolina.

ND: Growing up, I didn't know anyone who was gay. I was actually one of one or two "girls" at my public high school who had short hair. So it was something that people asked about a lot. I had a lot of fear around it—like, "This is just not allowed," or "Is this even something where happiness is possible? How could that be true when so many people in my life openly disdain gay people?"

In 2020, he wrote an illustrated coming-out story that was published in *Oprah Daily*. "It wasn't that being gay had never occurred to me," he wrote. "It just didn't fit in my conception of myself, and so my brain did its best to edit it out entirely." He'd learned his value to be intrinsically tied to marriage and male desire. "Being gay would mean that I had failed at being desired by men—which meant that I was worthless as a woman. There's a very Evangelical idea that true happiness is not possible outside of God's Plan for Your Life, and you will always feel a void in your soul that something is missing."

ND, photographed by Molly.

"The fight to come out was not so much that I was dealing with a very, very unsupportive family," he explains to me. "It was fighting against things that I had always assumed were true."

ND: In the same way that I thought I couldn't live a fulfilled life as a non-Christian—that there would never be any true joy in my life if I wasn't specifically devoted to serving Christ—I also assumed that there'd never be any real joy in my life if I didn't end up with a man. That was something that took a really, really long time to reprogram.

I still had this idea that I'm gonna end up in South Carolina again, married to a man, with kids in the church. Even transitioning has been like, "Well, I want top surgery, but what if I have to be a soccer mom?" Why would I think that at this point? Why is that still in my head?

There's a lot of pain in rewiring—it is a very uncomfortable process. And I think that even people who aren't raised Evangelical have versions of that. But it's a very messy process. And it can be a very ugly process. It can be a very painful process. And so for me, even though being queer has only brought me joy—and everything about this is making my life bigger and making me more capable of joy—the pain is still always a part of it.

MOLLY: Spending the time to sit with yourself and figure out what you want—that can feel very selfish. But it ultimately makes you a better part of your worlds.

Molly, photographed by ND.

ND: I just read *Stone Butch Blues* for the first time, and there's this part where coming out is described as like hurtling toward a cliff. And at a certain point, you cannot stop. You have to jump off that cliff and figure it out on the way down, which can be so terrifying. But there's a reason you can't stop. There's a reason you can't go back.

Trans people describe the process of having your egg cracked—once your egg starts breaking, you can't put it back together. Because it's not possible. You're growing larger as a person.

I really did think that if I left the church, if I came out as queer, I would be lost. I would be less capable of happiness. And I didn't realize how big my joy could get once I went hurtling off that cliff. I'm feeling the same way now again, with gender. I'm just like, "What is waiting for me here? Am I losing something?" And yet, every step I take is just like, "Oh, wow, I get to feel this way. Amazing."

Knowing that it's worked out in the past doesn't necessarily make it less scary. But it is something that I want people who are in the process of finding themselves to know: You can't go back at a certain point. This is you. I promise it's worth it.

One of the other impacts of growing up in an Evangelical community was that ND's access to pop culture virtually began and ended with educational homeschooling videos—*Muzzy*, the language-learning cartoon, was a favorite (they watched it in Spanish). But his parents did let him watch *Project Runway*. "It was creative," he says. "So I think that's why they let me."

ND: And there was a contestant, Kayne Gillaspie, who I was *in love with* and he's incredibly gay. He's got his little pixie hair and his cheek implants, and everything is glitter, everything is rainbow silk—the most stereotypically gay person that you can imagine. And I was like, "I must be in love with him. This is a crush." I knew(ish) what gay was, but I didn't really know how to recognize it in real life. And I remember realizing, "I don't think he likes women. I don't think this is a crush." And I think that was the first time it really clicked for me. This is a man who's gay and my connection with him is something different.

That moment can come from anywhere, I think, but it was this moment: realizing that there was something creating that connection that wasn't "I think you're handsome" or "I have a crush on you." It was something different.

MOLLY: That's so interesting. I can't remember what the big thing was, but I was very frightened of it. There was someone in my high school who identified as a lesbian, and they were really interested in me and asking my friends if I was queer, and I was just like, "Oh, my God, the fact that you even would register anything like that about me is terrifying."

I don't have a specific "ring of keys" moment, but I think it just was about always loving strong and capable women and having a lot of those in my life—especially being a teen and working at summer camp and having all these just cool women around me with boots and carabiners and stuff. Probably most of them were not queer—but just knowing this is the kind of person I connect with. And then as you start to go down that path, you're like, "A lot of these women are lesbians. Interesting."

ND: It's funny, now that I'm going on this gender journey, I feel like I'm having that with male celebrities I liked when I was younger. I'm just dressing exactly like this picture of Orlando Bloom I had on my wall.

Like so many people in this book, neither of them can recall any examples of happy queer love growing up. "I had a cousin who came out as gay," ND says. "And I just never saw him. He didn't come to any of the family events."

ND: I did have a queer mentor when I was twenty. I had an internship with a comics company here in LA, and my boss was a lesbian. I didn't think of it that way at the time, but seeing someone who was living her life that way was such an incredibly huge deal for me. I wish I'd had that a little younger. I wish I had been able to look at happy queer couples or happy out people I knew.

And like so many people in this book, they're very aware that they're able to be that for a new generation of queer kids.

MOLLY: It's cool to show younger fans—because we have so many younger fans—that you can be queer, and you can be in a happy relationship, and you can support and love each other. I think that sometimes has made me more comfortable sharing more than I would have thought I ever would, because I do want people to know that they can do that. There is actual happiness waiting for you as a queer adult.

But they also became famous, at least originally, online, in an environment that's notoriously difficult to draw boundaries in. "Our relationship with social media has become a little bit painful in the last couple years," Molly says. "And so we're trying to figure out the lines there."

ND: I've been stepping back a lot from social media in the last year just because I'm in a period of transition, in more ways than one. And sometimes, by voicing something, you put it in a box too early. I want to spend time with myself. I want to do things that feel real and right to me, not just because it's something that plays into people's perceptions of me on social media—or is actively trying to change the way that people view me on social media. That can sometimes get in the way of genuine growth.

It is important to us to be out. It is important for us to have our relationship be visible and show that certain things are possible—existing in the world as a queer human. But I also think that there is a lot of value in being quiet and stepping back. And taking time to really explore something or learn something before living it out very publicly.

However they're putting their actual, real-life selves out there, their work still speaks for them, and it continues to be undeniably queer—the kinds of queer stories that remind us that "coming out" is only one stage in our big, beautiful queer lives.

"As a storyteller, when I started dating ND, I realized that queer love is different than straight love," Molly says. Not simply practical differences. "The feelings are different; the arcs of the relationship are different. It's all its own thing."

MOLLY: That became something that I really wanted to put into stories. I want to write specifically queer stories with very queer feelings that you don't see in straight stories.

They both deliberately avoid the stories that are usually so essentialized for queer people. "I do not like incorporating homophobia into the stories that I tell," ND says. "Stories about homophobia can quickly get very painful in a way that's not always rewarding." Instead, he tells more universal stories that evoke those same feelings—"two people fighting for something that is not a given, something that other people don't want for them or are trying actively to keep them away from."

And because of that, their stories explore the nuances of queer experiences in a way that many queer narratives don't. "I remember when we were getting together," Molly says, "and I had this interesting feeling of almost stepping outside of heteronormativity, where I am suddenly not a part of this thing that matters so much to so many people. You're afraid to step out of it, but then once you step out, you're like, 'Oh, my god, there's this whole other big world.' I'm so excited to put that world into stories now."

ANTHONY HEMINGWAY

(HE/HIM)
DIRECTOR

STEVEN NORFLEET

(HE/HIM)
ACTOR

"WE ACTUALLY MET AT CHURCH," Steven tells me, grinning. It was Easter Sunday 2014. They each went to the service with friends that day. Anthony turned to his friend Draco and mentioned that he was interested in meeting the cute boy with the wide smile outside of the church. "To this day, we thank him for being the one to bring us together," Steven says. In true LA style, "he says he wants his ten percent."

But nothing happened that day. Steven was a dancer at the time and was headed out on tour; Anthony had just come off directing a series of episodes for David Simon's *Treme* and was getting ready to head back to Louisiana to shoot *Underground*. But they stayed on each other's radar.

STEVEN: We were texting, flirting back and forth. And before I even knew he was a producer and director, I knew him as this guy that threw these massive parties in LA. New Year's was around the corner, and I asked him if he was doing a New Year's party. He said no.

But a couple days later, Steven got a text with a flyer for Anthony's New Year's party. "Best party of my life," Steven says.

STEVEN: We keep talking till maybe two thirty in the morning. Everybody's about to go home, but I want to keep talking—and I don't want him to think that I want to talk about . . . something else. But I go for it.

Anthony was giving onesies as Christmas gifts that year, so he had a whole box of them at his house. They opened a bottle of wine, slipped into some onesies, and eventually fell asleep. "We've been rocking ever since."

I ask Anthony if the party only happened because Steven asked about it. "Absolutely," he says without hesitation. "I had no plans and no desire." The best party of Steven's life? Anthony threw it together in a couple days.

It's that same skill set—pulling all the right people together in the right moment—that makes him so good at his job. He's a director and producer who's worked on shows like *Orange Is the New Black*, *The Wire*, and *The People v. O. J. Simpson*. He's been nominated for an Emmy, a Golden Globe, a BAFTA, and an NAACP Image Award.

STEVEN: He really is the captain of the ship—when it comes to every project that he's a part of.
            When we first got together, it was shocking to me to understand how busy he was. In my previous relationships, we were able to communicate day in, day out. And when we got together, that changed drastically—and my mind is thinking all types of reasons why he's not texting me back or returning my call.
            But then, when he was working in Baton Rouge, I flew out there. And I got to see firsthand why he's so busy. He really understands all the different jobs that come with making a TV show or movie. And because he really understands it all, he's able to have his input—he understands how to have the heart and the mind as if he is a part of the makeup department or the hair department or the camera department. And he really cares for everybody, whether it be the lead actor on the call sheet or the extras on set. He really makes sure everybody feels that they're necessary to make this project come to life.

And since that visit, Steven has had the chance to experience that himself. He pivoted from dancing to acting in 2016, and after a five-episode arc on HBO's *Watchmen*, he played the heartbreaking Paul de Pointe du Lac on the new, queerer *Interview with a Vampire* series. But he's also shared sets with Anthony: He was in an episode of *Power* that Anthony directed, and they worked together on *Genius*, the Aretha Franklin biopic.

ANTHONY: I love watching him stretch himself. I love watching him learn more about himself, find new dimensions of himself—dimensions that I see in him. And I love watching him explore the characters that he takes on—and allowing himself to transport into places that I know may be uncomfortable for him. But seeing the result of it is the beauty. I hear him connect to and learn more even about himself and just growing in ways that affect him personally, not only in the workspace but also in a personal space. So I just love watching him allow himself to really explore these spaces that challenge him.

A few weeks before I interviewed Steven and Anthony, Billie and I decided to watch *Interview with a Vampire*. At the time, we didn't realize that Steven was in it. The main character is Louis de Pointe du Lac—a gay Black man in New Orleans in the early 1900s who falls in love with a vampire and, eventually, becomes one himself. Steven plays his brother, Paul, a "troubled" young man who joined the priesthood; he knows his brother is gay and frets for his immortal soul. The characters' love for each other is tangible. And at the end of the first episode, as the brothers watch the sunrise from their roof, Paul steps off the edge and kills himself.

We'd known the character for an hour, and Billie and I were devastated. When I tell Steven, he replies, "So far, the best job I've ever had."

ANTHONY: I knew that was coming, but I still was gutted.

STEVEN: The day we shot it was very hard. When you're shooting TV, you can shoot the same thing five, six, seven times. And he'd have to fall off the roof. As soon as they cut, the guy who plays Louis—Jacob Anderson—and I would just find each other. And we would just cuddle. Because we both understood what this moment was for us as characters and as people.

But I had to find beauty in making that choice. Because that's who Paul was. Paul didn't see him ending his life as a bad thing in that moment. He saw it as going to the next chapter of his life.

I ask him what it was like to play a character that struggled so much with his brother's homosexuality.

STEVEN: Sometimes, opportunities come to me only because I'm a part of the LGBTQ community. And I am grateful that those opportunities are there, but I don't want to just be seen as that. This job allows me to transform into different people, and I won't always have to play who I am in my everyday life.

I completely understood Paul. Some roles can be different, as far as how you prepare, but for me, I wanted to be Paul day in and day out. And what I love about being an actor—I believe there's something inside of you that can connect to every single role. And once you find that connection, you're able to make that person that

I WAS LIKE, "MOM, I'M GAY. I HOPE YOU STILL LOVE ME." AND SHE PULLED ME TIGHTER AND UTTERED THE WORDS VERBATIM: "OF COURSE I LOVE YOU. YOU'RE WHO GOD MADE YOU TO BE."

—*Anthony Hemingway*

much more real. It really gave me joy, and a [platform] to just have fun and learn about who this character is and what I could bring to the table.

ANTHONY: It was fun watching him really take that on because he devoted himself to learning about Catholicism; he had to learn how to tap. Just to watch his dedication and passion for it was really awesome. And, you know, he would go to the cathedral and New Orleans—

STEVEN: Mass every day.

TOP IMAGE:
Anthony,
photographed by
Steven.

RIGHT IMAGE:
Steven,
photographed by
Anthony.

Neither of them are Catholic, so Mass was a new world. But they met at church for a reason—it's been deeply entwined in both of their lives. Knowing that, I ask if either of them had access to any queer role models or characters or examples growing up.

STEVEN: I remember being in my grandmother's house. I was watching *Rent*, and I remember it was dark. And me and musicals can kind of be hit-or-miss sometimes, but the music of *Rent* was just fire. And I was just loving it, all of it. And I remember the moment where the guy and Angel come off the train, and they're singing and jollying and coming down the street. And I'm still very much entertained. And I recognize that there's a connection between these two. But I'm still not really thinking much of it, because I've never seen two men—or anybody of our rainbow community—be intimate onscreen.

And I remember seeing the moment that they kiss, and I was mind-blown. Because it was that moment, I felt, we were tapping into a new space within TV and film—seeing two people within the rainbow community be able to express their love in such a joyous way onscreen.

I was brought up in Detroit, Michigan, and I felt being gay was wrong. And the word *gay* wasn't necessarily tied to who you were sexually attracted to. It was more of a word to demean someone else, to make somebody else feel bad. Seeing them—they made me feel like, "Wait a minute—there are people out there that I can connect with." It gave me the hope that, if they're doing this in a movie, maybe this community is a lot bigger than I'm imagining. And maybe right now, there's no one around me that I can relate to. But it gave me hope that as I get older, maybe I can find people that I can connect with and possibly even fall in love. *Rent* was the light bulb for me.

I graduated high school, went to college at Morehouse College in Atlanta, Georgia. And Atlanta is a city full of Black queer men. And at the time, I wasn't aware of it. But I'm meeting more of these people within this community while I was at school, and that got me to open up a little bit, which then got me to feel comfortable to tell my best friends back in Detroit. But still yet, if a stranger was asking, I would have said no.

And then he met Anthony.

STEVEN: And my family still doesn't know. And I'm realizing I could marry this man, and I think I will be robbing my family of that opportunity to truly know who I am. I can be completely married to a whole man, and they could have no idea. That was an option that I was considering.

I decided, "You know what, Steve, let's take the risk. Tell your family and see what happens." And I knew there were definitely *thoughts* about homosexuality coming from my parents, coming from my aunts and uncles and sisters and brothers, that made me a bit more scared to come out. But I found myself getting to a point of being comfortable: If they accept me, cool; if they don't, cool. At this point, I'm living in LA; we've been together for some time. And I feel very confident that this is my guy for the rest of time. And if my family chose not to embrace us, embrace him, I was okay with starting a new world with him and the ones that loved us in LA.

When I told my family, most of them were cool. Some of them weren't. But I was okay. Because even if some of them didn't agree with my choice of who I want to spend the rest of my life with, they did respect him. And they respected me as a person.

I went through a time of my life where I wasn't completely sure if homosexuality was okay, according to the Bible, because I grew up in the church as well, and I was taught that this was a bad thing. So when it came to those family members, I didn't fault them for it, because I was once at that place myself.

I ask him how he got from point A to point B—from believing that his queerness was wrong to accepting himself for who he was.

STEVEN: I was in college. And this was the moment where I really accepted Christ into my life. And in that, I went gung ho about saying I wasn't listening to certain things, I was watching certain things, I only wanted to do what I felt was right, according to the Word.

Within that journey, it got extremely hard. It didn't make sense—why something that was coming so natural to me was considered wrong. And the way I feel about my beliefs is, what's considered wrong or right—there's a reason why to it. "Thou shalt not kill" makes sense to me because killing people hurts people, hurts the loved ones around you. But I couldn't really understand why me loving another man was wrong. And I kept trying to figure out these different reasons and never could find one.

I still truly do believe in God. I still go to church; I still read my Bible. I do believe that this bond, this love that we have, is totally acceptable, that God is totally over us. He's in between us. He's totally in our lives as a couple, as individuals. And once I got to that place, that was a turning point for me realizing, Steve, it's okay to embrace that true love when it comes, and you can still be a God-fearing man.

Steven stops for a second and looks over at Anthony. "Your turn to talk."

ANTHONY: Well, we're thirteen years apart. I'm a seventies baby—grew up in New York City. So I saw queer people around me my entire life. I also grew up in the church but at an early age found my relationship with spirituality versus the religion and understanding that the representation of that God is love. And to me, it's all about love and your heart. And so, I think I accepted myself before I found the confidence to come out because I still was unsure. We all want to be loved and live a life that's harmonious and get along with everyone.

When I was twenty-five, I came out, and the most important person for me was my mother. I'm basically a preacher's kid. My family is very churchy. My mother is a minister now. So that was the thing that was always riding over me—just wanting to make sure that my mother loved me and my family loved me.

I made the decision for myself to live my truth because I knew I wasn't a mistake. And I knew I wasn't doing the wrong thing. Because, you know, of course, I grew up questioning all those things. I prayed that if this is so wrong, take it out of my thoughts, my mind, my heart, all of it. And it just was *of* me. So, I just knew that I was who I was supposed to be. And that was the confirmation that my mother gave me when I came out to her when I was twenty-five. I gave her a hug and I was like, "Mom, I'm gay. I hope you still love me." And she pulled me tighter and uttered the words verbatim: "Of course I love you. You're who God made you to be."

STEVEN: And I want to add on to that—what I think is so important, that I feel a lot of people within the rainbow community are missing, is that I think when it comes to God's love, we get so harped on about what we're not supposed to be doing and forgetting that we're supposed to be leading with love. Regardless of how you feel about homosexuality, whether you agree with it or not, whether you feel God is okay with it or not, I think one thing we all can agree on is that God loves his children. And I think people put that thought third or fourth or fifth and try to focus on the things that you're not supposed to be doing, or what God may consider as a no-no, when we need to be leading with the fact that, regardless, God loves you.

Then he turns to Anthony again. "Do you remember the first queer person you saw?"

ANTHONY: My cousin—an older cousin of mine—has been loud and proud my entire life.

He lives in South Brooklyn, and he's my mother and father's age. So I grew up watching him be very confident and comfortable in his skin. But of course, it also came with hearing all the small talk—even in the family—of how so many people don't agree.

But I always found encouragement in his strength and confidence. And that was something that I never forgot.

We talk a lot about the stigma, the shame, the acceptance—just even the humanity that we want to help contribute to. Contributing to the positive growth of the queer community—and the intersectionality of being Black and queer—to be a part of that representation means a lot to us.

One of the first things I read about Anthony and Steven was their *New York Times* wedding announcement. It was a huge spread with the headline "Our Love Is Built to Last." Considering Anthony's reputation for lavish parties, I ask them, surely there's a good proposal story.

ANTHONY: Steven is a person who likes simplicity in a lot of things. I'm the bigger, more boisterous, grander one. Everything's a production. It's very aligned with who I am, my professional career, and just who I am personally too. I love people. I love energy and just having fun and creating moments. And so it had gotten to a point in our relationship where we'd had conversations about marriage—making sure that we both wanted it—and I remember we were in New York walking around one day. We were in the Meatpacking District and walked past a couple of jewelry shops. And we said, "Let's go in here. Let's check it out." You know, so we went in. And it was at a time where we were thinking, if we get married, what kind of rings do we want? You know, let's just throw that out there.

So, we walked into a jewelry shop in the Meatpacking District. And it was really wild, because we both landed on the rings that we wear now at the same time. It was like the first ring we saw. It spoke to us in so many ways. Our rings basically are two halves—they're like two crowns. It's like two kings coming together to make one. They interlock. And so we saw them. And then it was like, "Oh, what's your ring size? What's your ring size?" And so we get all that done. We get our ring finger sizes and then just keep moving on throughout the day.

Two years after that, he was coming up on his thirtieth birthday, and I had a moment I can't ever forget. I was shooting in New Orleans, Louisiana, doing the pilot to *The Purge*. And I'm sitting in my office one day before we started shooting, and I had this loaded, visceral moment that I just started crying.

STEVEN: I don't think I know this one!

ANTHONY: Because I had been thinking about proposing. It really started with thinking about his birthday. It was his thirtieth. Again—[*points to Steven*] Mr. Simplicity, [*points to himself*] Mr. Big. I want to do everything. I'm trying to convince him: You only turn thirty once; this has to be crazy and big. All this to sway him and convince him to do more than what he wants to do.

And I was thinking about the birthday party. And then in a moment, I just erupted in tears. And it was just because it was the moment that I really sat and

thought, and I was like, "I'm going to do it. I'm gonna propose to him on his birthday." And I sat there; I had a moment; I shed some tears. And I was like, "Okay, okay." I talked to the guy at the jewelry shop—he remembered who I was and still had a record of our ring sizes. And so I ordered the rings that day, and then I started crying even more; it was great. Like, "Oh, my God, this is happening; like, this is really happening."

And of course, my greatest challenge was the party and convincing him not to do something small and intimate.

He succeeded: He threw a party with nearly a hundred friends on a yacht in Marina del Rey—and he rented a school bus to take everyone to and from the party. ("We didn't want anyone drinking and driving.")

ANTHONY: My heart is completely beating out of my chest, because I know the moment is coming. My head is sticking out the window trying to get air because I'm like, "Oh, my God, it's coming." So I kind of tailored it into just making a speech about his birthday. And one of my best friends had the ring. And of course, now I'm starting to tear up, and I know the room is all on me because they are all waiting for this to happen—which made it even worse for me. So I'm a wreck, starting to say how much he means to me and how much I love him. And I look at my friend and I give her the sign. And she starts to walk to me. And I can see him now starting to see what's happening. And now I see him, like, start to connect the dots. So I quickly got to the moment—got down on my knee and asked him the question, and we both boo-hooed, and then he turned around and then proposed to me.

Steven has been quiet through this whole story.

STEVEN: Let me give you some of my perspective—because I'm the one that's all the way in the dark.

I think now I am realizing more where my love for simplicity comes from. I think it reminds me of my upbringing. Life wasn't really grand. And some of my favorite moments growing up are very simple moments. Being with my best friends. And we're chilling in somebody's living room, eating Little Caesars pizza. And for me, the simplicity is more about not needing other things to make this moment a good time but just the people that you surround yourself with.

So when it came to my thirtieth birthday, I really only wanted the people that I truly am close with. Right? That's—that was three people. So I wanted a sailboat.

And it'd be about five, six of us on the boat. And I was totally fine with that. Right? He talks me out of it. Shows me the boat. And I'm like, "This is too much. I don't even want to invite this many people to fill this boat."

Then, on top of that, he's telling me the people that's coming. And I'm in my head going, "Interesting. I would have never thought of them to come to my thirtieth birthday, but whatever." But nothing is coming together with me thinking this is an engagement moment.

He noticed something was weird when he first went up to the bar.

STEVEN: It's my thirtieth. I'm walking up, asking, "Where are the shots? Let's do this. Let's go." And all of my friends keep trying to take drinks away from me and give me food, and I'm getting frustrated. "No, we should be drinking. Why am I doing this alone? Why do they keep taking my drinks from my hand?"

It really didn't click until I saw him reach out and his friend gave him the ring.

Their engagement rings were the bottom crowns of the interlocking sets they'd seen together in New York. When they got married at Newhall Mansion in California, overlooking the Santa Clara River Valley, they gave each other the upper set of interlocking crowns.

STEVEN: Again, I wanted a simple wedding. Now I would have wanted a bit more than three people—but I still want it simple. But my only thing was where we got married. Because we went to a friend's wedding at Newhall Mansion—it's a castle. And once we got there, I said, "If we do it, this has got to be the place."

So I said, "Okay, this could be the place." But of course, he took it and changed it dramatically. And it really worked out because the guy who runs Newhall Mansion, we kind of was scratching each other's backs because he wanted to do so much. As far as construction and all these flowers—

I interrupt. Construction?

STEVEN: He literally had a dance floor built.

The wedding was a proper Anthony Hemingway affair. The ceremony was on the estate's front steps. The railings were wrapped in lavender and orchids and bay leaves. There were costume changes and a gospel choir dressed in white and chairs that looked like thrones. They had more than three hundred guests, including Regina King, Andre Royo, Sterling K. Brown, and Sarah Paulson. The way they tell it, even the *New York Times* photographer had so much fun, he stayed for the whole event. The headline, "Our Love Is Built to Last," was a quote from Anthony's vows. "I will face it all with you," he

Self-portrait by Steven and Anthony.

continued. "Together, we will ask God to keep us sensitive to each other's spirit. I will love you forever; we will become veterans in love together."

When we met them in LA, they'd been married for almost four years. In that time, they'd adopted Blue, their steely gray French bulldog, and weathered a pandemic. During lockdown, they both rediscovered their love for tennis, and it got them through some of the longest months, so they decide they want to do their photo shoot at a tennis club.

They arrive at the country club in matching sweatshirts that read "Two Kings, One Castle"— swag from their wedding. (A couple weeks later, a package arrives at our house with two swag bags of our own.) Within a few minutes, an older Black man hollers, "It's always nice to see some chocolate around here!" And from the neighboring court, a woman asks Steven, "Is there really room for two kings in one castle?"

He patiently answers her. "Yes, of course there is," he says, smiling over at Anthony.

SAMANTHA BEAIRD

(SHE/HER)
RESEARCH AND
DEVELOPMENT
CHEF AT CANLIS

AISHA IBRAHIM

(SHE/HER)
EXECUTIVE
CHEF AT CANLIS

"I WENT 99.9 PERCENT OF THE WAY IN FOR A KISS, and I just stopped and went back to my room," Aisha says, hand over her mouth.

This was back in 2016, and Aisha was on the coast of Thailand—just north of Phuket. Michelin-starred chef Eneko Atxa had asked her to run his restaurant at a resort in the beach town of Phang Nga. ("Not horrible," she says, laughing.) A few months after she had arrived, the restaurant was recognized as the number one up-and-coming restaurant in Southeast Asia. Then suddenly, her sous chef left the country, leaving her in desperate need of help in the kitchen. "And so overnight, my inbox is filled with all these young cooks from all over the world who are like, 'I'm from Copenhagen,' or 'I'm from Mexico City, and I want to come and work on the beach in Thailand,'" she says.

One of the first résumés she opened was Samantha Beaird's, a chef from San Francisco's James Beard Award–winning Boulevard with a food science background and experience in recipe development at America's Test Kitchen. Aisha didn't respond quickly, so Samantha slid into her DMs. ("I definitely left her on read for a few days, before I realized that was a thing," Aisha admits.)

Samantha arrived in Phang Nga in February 2016. They were both from the Bay Area and the only two native English speakers in the kitchen. When Samantha first arrived, she needed to visit the consulate on a regular basis to get her paperwork in order. The nearest town was a forty-five-minute drive away, and "Aisha was the only one offering a ride," she says.

Because there was only one road to the consulate, they often ended up spending hours in the car. "She just asked me about my life," Aisha says. "And I was like, 'Wow, we get along really well.'" Over time, Samantha started asking questions like, "Say, have you ever dated your boss before?"

One night, they went out to dinner at a restaurant that Aisha normally went to when she was treating herself alone. "The owner, who I'd become friends with, leans over and is just like, 'She's gorgeous.' And I was like, 'Thank you, Sean. I'm so glad I got your approval. We're actually just on a friend date.'"

But that night, when they got back to the resort, was the night she leaned in 99.9 percent of the way for a kiss.

SAMANTHA: It was funny. I went back to my room, and she left a water for an apology. It was very, very cute.

AISHA: A bottle of really nice water outside of her door. I did not know what else to do. So I went back to my room and I sulked.

SAMANTHA: The next time we hung out, you had more confidence.

AISHA: And we've been together ever since.

"We've visited fourteen countries," Aisha says. "There was a year where we took fifty flights. We've lived in Singapore and Thailand—we temporarily lived in Taiwan. And I don't know how many restaurants that we opened and worked in. We've been all over the world for the last five years."

Until 2021, when they landed in Seattle. On May 3, a *New York Times* headline declared, "Canlis Hires Its First Female Executive Chef." The restaurant—a seventy-year-old institution owned by three generations of white men—had only had six chefs before Aisha. It'd become a name in the national dining scene in the last few decades, but when the restaurant opened in 1950, it was credited with "creating Pacific Northwest cuisine," serving surf-and-turf classics from its perch on a cliff over Lake Union with a view of the Cascades.

I would have assumed that the restaurant's very white, very male, very colonial history would be a quick turnoff for Samantha and Aisha. The founder, Peter Canlis, had moved to Oahu right before World War II and cooked at the Pearl Harbor USO before running a restaurant in Honolulu called the Broiler. There, he worked primarily with Japanese people, and when he opened Canlis, he had all of the servers wear kimonos (a uniform that lasted well into the '90s).

But Samantha and Aisha had an unexpected perspective on the institution.

SAMANTHA: My grandma is Japanese, and my dad came over in 1955 from Japan. And I know his stories of being Japanese in the US during that time—it was very hard. And so for me, the idea of someone [celebrating Japanese culture] was very bold and very progressive in some ways. It's kind of wild.

AISHA: In the context of the time frame, that's insane.
                          And in Japanese work culture—especially restaurant culture—they believe in an all-team responsibility. I worked in Japan, and there is no differentiation of front of house and back of house. If the dining room team needs help, the kitchen steps up. We will walk the guests to their seats; we will walk the guests to their car. There was no such thing as "you get more of a cut because of where you work." So the theory is that, because of the number of Japanese folks who worked on staff at the time it opened, Canlis might be the first restaurant to share a tip pool in America.

However progressive Canlis was in 1950, though, in 2020 their kitchen had never had a female head chef, and it had certainly never seen a chef like Aisha before—a queer, Filipina, immigrant woman from a Muslim family with a background in Basque and Japanese cooking. She was quickly declared "a cause for all kinds of celebration."

In the same article that announced Aisha's new role, the *Times* announced Samantha's as well: "Ms. Ibrahim's partner, Samantha Beaird, will join the staff at Canlis, too, in the newly created position of research and development chef." It put a formal name on a dynamic they'd had for the last five years.

"In the past, it's just been the two of us," Samantha says. To prepare for a dinner service in Thailand, they would go to a market and find whatever ingredients excited them.

SAMANTHA: Aisha would dive deep into "What is the name of the ingredient? What is the plant? How does it grow?" And I would dive into "What is the functionality of the ingredient? And what kind of cool things can we do with it?"

Her job, essentially, was to discover every unique function that ingredient could offer their menu.

AISHA: Some of the proudest things we were able to serve, even in Thailand, you'd put something down in front of a guest, and you'd say, "This has taken about three years to get to this point." It's a very long-term way of thinking about food and sustainability and how to create something that is different but also so intentional.

One of their prix fixe Canlis menus included a Walla Walla onion broth that took days to make and a piece of kampachi aged for seventy-two hours in kohlrabi. Samantha regularly visits Washington State University's Bread Lab, where they breed new varieties of grains that are healthier, more affordable, and more sustainable. They grind their grains in-house, and this flour makes a rye loaf that's unlike anything I've put in my mouth.

SAMANTHA: We don't like to use chemicals or additives in food, so it's really fun to pull those properties out of natural ingredients and use that instead. You can see the scientific reason, but you can also see that people from different cultures are using [these foods] this way.

The best example might be their tempura batter. Typically, chefs will add a powder called methylcellulose to the mixture to help it bind to the food better and keep it crispy. In Sri Lanka, people traditionally put okra in their batter. Turns out, Samantha learned, that same chemical naturally occurs in okra. So now in their kitchen, instead of a white powder, they use pureed okra to perfect the texture. "It's about seeing what people from different cultures are using, and combining everything into one place where we can extract that knowledge and learn and grow," Samantha says.

She and Aisha invited us to the restaurant for dinner in the spring. When the server showed us to our table, she explained that we were at table number one—Peter Canlis's original desk, where he would take meetings and survey the restaurant during service. His original phone sat next to us. "It still works," she warned. "It might ring."

A few minutes later, Aisha called us from the host station, giggling, before she popped out to say hello. She and Samantha served several of the courses—explaining how they'd made a breading out of Walla Walla onion, or a palate cleanser with frozen yogurt, blood orange, olive oil, and sea salt.

Their food hardly resembles the filet mignon and lobster classics that made Canlis famous in the '50s. (Though Aisha did concede to keeping the Canlis Salad on the menu; it's the only holdout. "It's a reminder of how far the restaurant has come," she told *Art Culinaire*.)

When we visited Canlis with them on their off hours, it was clear that kitchen is their space. Samantha will sometimes deliberately get to work early to sit quietly in the kitchen with Aisha, breaking down whole fish. (They'll even mark certain fish as "for chef" so no one beats them to it.) They parallel each other—from the moment they set up the knives and towels to the cleanup at the end.

Seeing the way they move through the kitchen—and the world—it seems markedly harmonious. But they did have at least one hurdle to getting there.

SAMANTHA: I'd never really had any feelings [for other women]. And when I started having feelings for Aisha, I was just like, "Well, I fell in love with a person. And that's amazing. She's a person and that's what matters." I've never put myself into the category of bi or lesbian because I didn't have any of those feelings beforehand, so I still don't know if that's me.

AISHA: And it's definitely a source of tension. Because my closest friends, all of them were either bi or queer or *proudly* lesbian, *proudly* gay, and were like, "You are thirty years old. You do not venture into this type of relationship. This person has never been with a woman before, your career is taking off right now, and you need someone who knows themself and who knows you and can love you." And so there was a lot of tension around that from her family and from my friends, and I think, even as recently as like a couple years ago, it made me feel like, "Should you be gay? Should you have an identity?" But now I'm like, "I think you should just be what you want to be," you know?

SAMANTHA: I think it's not inconsistent, also, with my personality in general.

AISHA: You're a chameleon. But you're also just you. Uniquely you.

Honestly, it took me a while to accept that she was not comfortable within a frame of "identity." And I had to ask myself, "Hey, Aisha, how long did it take you to be comfortable as a queer person? How long did it take you to be comfortable with the way that your name sounds, or being able to openly and proudly identify as someone who immigrated into this country? There's so many parts of identity that I feel like I had to learn to grow into. It took me my whole life. And so I think, to put this pressure on her, in a matter of months, a year, or even a few years—maybe I'm the one who's being unfair, and I'm the one who needs to understand that this person has a right to whatever their path is.

The beginning of their relationship also happened in a bubble. In Thailand, they had an entire ocean between them and the friends and family that might push a label on their relationship. And as foreigners in the country, they were afforded a more progressive attitude than their Thai counterparts.

"On the surface, Thailand is very, very open to the LGBTQ community, which is great on paper," Samantha says. And because, as foreigners, they didn't have any of the Thai cultural expectations foisted on them, they were able to exist pretty comfortably.

Mostly, at least. "It's not legally possible to marry there," Aisha says. "So we technically couldn't quarantine together."

When they got back to the States in 2021, they had to integrate their relationship into the worlds they'd left behind. Because this was Samantha's first relationship with a woman, she had a hard time figuring out how to introduce Aisha to her family. "I wanted my family to get to know Aisha," she says. "And not as this person that is coming in and completely changing my whole family's view of who they raised."

AISHA: I can recall some really funny conversations from the beginning, because her family members didn't know right away. Her mom was getting married, so I volunteered to cook for her wedding. And it was maybe a couple months into our relationship and her cousin pulled me aside and was like, "You guys are together, right?"

And her [cousin's] mom—who, we all love her, Auntie Dodo is very honest. And in the middle of dinner that night, she was like, "I dated a woman in the seventies"— as I was dropping the roasted chicken [at the table] during the wedding—and she's like, "And it was a great time of my life." And the whole table was just laughing because they were all trying to get us to say something. And I was like, "That's a great anecdote. I'm gonna go and grab my wine."

Samantha is still unclear on whether or not she took the right approach with her family. "In some ways, it was a good way to go about it," she says. "In some ways, it was not." She says now that, in a way, it negated their relationship—effectively asking Aisha to temporarily tuck herself back in the closet.

SAMANTHA: Obviously, it didn't take long for people to figure it out. And my dad was very accepting. He was very like, "I just want you to be happy, whatever you need. Whatever you want."

AISHA: Your dad didn't miss a beat!

SAMANTHA: He's just, "I'm glad you're happy. I love you both; I just want you to be happy," you know? But not everyone is . . . that way. So there's definitely been some hard conversations.

It was a difficult needle to thread for Aisha, who had come out as a teenager in conservative, white West Virginia and had consistently seen the value in being out and being proud.

AISHA: I came out in high school. I came out at a Catholic all-girls school and brought a woman as my date to prom. And the sisters were like, "We're so glad you go to this school." And I was like, "Wow! I thought they would have been so conservative."

Self-portrait taken by Aisha and Samantha.

During my time there, I got a handwritten letter, anonymously, from a seventh-grader that was like, "I think I'm bi, and I'm so glad that you are a senior here. You have helped me." I still carry the weight of that letter today.

After high school, she moved from West Virginia to the Bay Area to go to culinary school. "I was so lucky," she says. "The person who was our housing residence director, that I just happened to become friends with, was the managing director for Dinah Shore." For the uninitiated—and those who've never seen the original *L Word* series—the Dinah Shore Weekend is the world's largest lesbian and queer femme event, and it's held in Palm Springs every year.

AISHA: After she hired me as an RA at school, she was like, "You're family, right?" And I was like, "Yes." And she was like, "Oh, my God, I'm gonna take you under my wing." And so I immediately felt connected to community. And I know, still to this day, that that was so impactful for me in so many positive ways. She gave me the opportunity to work Dinah Shore in its heyday, when *The L Word* and everything was happening. And I grew up getting to know pop queer culture in that way. And celebrate it.

I had no access to that as a kid. And so to be able to grow into an adult, and own it, and be proud of it, and then be in the community myself. Huge. And so now I get this awesome responsibility to do something really positive—with this job. And to look back on how just isolated I felt in that moment, until now, to where I'm standing, and that's why I see it as such an amazing golden opportunity to bring people up or bring people along and say, "Hey, it's okay. You've got a whole community here."

They've settled into the suburbs of Seattle, just east of Lake Washington. "We literally live on a cul-de-sac," Aisha says. "It's so weird." For their photo shoot, they decided to go to Canlis, naturally, but first we meet them at a sprawling six-hundred-acre park where they take their dog, Mochi, to run. She's a curly-haired black-and-white flying pile of limbs—and incredibly good at finding the nearest mud pit. (Since we met up with them, they've adopted Mochi's little sister, Dashi.)

They got married later that year; the ceremony was on a ferry in the Puget Sound, midtransit, on its way to Whidbey Island. When they came ashore, they had a dinner on a farm that was catered by the Seattle Filipino restaurant Musang (whose chef, Melissa Miranda, was named one of the best new chefs in America in 2022). The meal was called a "kamayan"—a communal feast that was served family style, on one long table, with the food presented on broad banana leaves and eaten with your hands.

When Canlis announced Aisha and Samantha's wedding, the owners, Mark and Brian Canlis (the grandsons of Peter Canlis), referred to the couple as "the stewards of this place and our people." And it's very much how Aisha and Samantha move through the kitchen as a whole. Their presence hasn't just transformed the menu at Canlis; it's expanded the types of people who feel like they have a place in their dining room.

SAMANTHA: The dining room staff has told us that there are so many more people of color in the dining room now.

AISHA: They're like, "I feel like our audience is shifting, chef." I've had people message me and be like, "I've never been to Canlis before. And I've lived in Seattle my whole life. And I'm Filipino, or I'm queer, and I just made my first reservation."

The back of the house is similarly diverse, and—also in the name of stewardship—they take pride in running theirs as a "learning kitchen." It's a benefit of having Samantha as one of the leaders in the kitchen.

AISHA: It combats the things that we used to hate about being a cook. When you're growing up as a cook working in fine dining, very often you come across chefs who are like, "I don't have time to tell you why; just do it that way." We talked about how much we hated that. So why don't we have a learning kitchen? Samantha has the ability to tell the cooks, "You want to put it in this solution because of X, Y, and Z. This prevents oxidation because of the scientific property of blah, blah, blah." Having a food scientist on our team who's also a chef is cool.

As stewards of this old-school, classic institution, they clearly approach their roles deliberately and thoughtfully but also with a certain lightness. "I'm so excited that I get to carry this responsibility," Aisha says. She knows that in standing at the helm of a restaurant like Canlis, people could see her through the lens of any one of her identities—queer, Filipina, immigrant. "It's a tremendous opportunity—a powerful one to have in 2021," she says. "I hope that I can help people see strength in these identities."

ARE YOU SISTERS?

"PEOPLE THINK THAT WE'RE SISTERS," Mackenzie Scott tells me.

"It happens all the time," Jenna Gribbon says. Jenna is a painter best known for her portraits. Lately, they're all of Mackenzie, her wife. They're always painted from Jenna's perspective: Sometimes their legs are tangled together, other times Mackenzie is alone. She's almost always undressed. "In fact, there was one post from my most recent show in London, and it was all these paintings of Mackenzie, with our limbs entwined. You can see our bodies and our anatomy and whatever. And someone was like, 'These are paintings of the artist and her husband.'"

It seems to be an almost universal experience—having people refuse to perceive your queerness, even when it's the most obvious explanation for what's in front of them. There are Reddit threads and hashtags cataloging the countless waiters who have asked, "Are you sisters?" Billie and I have been asked if we're twins more than once (flip to our author photos if you want a good laugh). And we heard it in interview after interview—Ben and Daniel Barnz even named their production company We're Not Brothers.

"People can't wrap their heads around it," Mackenzie says. "People can't believe that women are in relationships with each other."

It's so common, in fact, that *Are You Two Sisters?* is the title of a book by lesbian sociologist Susan Krieger. The title was inspired by a moment with her partner outside of a bar in the New Mexican desert. She wrote: "A man followed me out, opening the door for me, offering to help me to my car. 'Are you two sisters?' he asked in a challenging tone as I stepped out of the dark bar and into the open air."

To her, the question alone encapsulates queer visibility and invisibility all in one. At the same time, it actively acknowledges that the people you're approaching are different from you but refuses to acknowledge their queerness. "The person who's asking you is settling their own discomfort," she says. "They want to place you."

The question unintentionally gets at the crux of one of the more nuanced parts of coming out. "You want to be seen," Susan says, "but it makes you vulnerable."

And it's part of what makes coming out an endless process. Every time a waiter asks if your wife is your sister, you have to decide: Do I want this person to know I'm queer? Does it feel safe? Or simply, do I want to be bothered?

In the first section of this book, many of the conversations explored what it means to look for yourself in others. In this section, the conversations explore what happens after that: deciding how you want to be seen—and how much.

Throughout this book, there are stories at every point along that spectrum. Barbara Belmont and Rochelle Diamond were married to men while they carried on wild lesbian affairs in the '70s, when neither of them felt safe to come out; during the same decade, Martha Nell Smith and Marilee Lindemann were staunchly out in their feminist graduate literature programs. Lydia Polgreen and Candy Feit quietly let people believe they were sisters when they worked abroad in places like India and West Africa, while Jenna Gribbon and Mackenzie Scott make vibrant, visceral, sexual art about each other, only to have critics assume one of them is a man.

The decision to be seen—to insist on being seen—ultimately defines why every one of these couples is in this book. "Over the course of my life, I've been through a really interesting transition," Lydia told us. "I was a reporter and a correspondent and wrote stories—and I think it was pretty easy for me in that work to be like, 'I'm just a byline. My personality doesn't matter.' And as I've stepped into more leadership positions, I think I've really questioned that perspective. It's become clear that it's really, really important that people who hold positions of power and are queer—or are Black or are nonbinary or whatever they are—hold that space . . . You can have power and you can shape the culture—you can shape the world."

IT'S PART OF WHAT
MAKES COMING OUT
AN ENDLESS PROCESS.
EVERY TIME A WAITER
ASKS IF YOUR WIFE
IS YOUR SISTER, YOU
HAVE TO DECIDE: DO I
WANT THIS PERSON TO
KNOW I'M QUEER?

JENNA GRIBBON

(SHE/HER)
PAINTER

MACKENZIE SCOTT, *AKA TORRES*

(SHE/HER)
MUSICIAN

THE FIRST TIME I talk to Mackenzie and Jenna, we're on Zoom, and their computer is carefully balanced on a green velour couch in their living room in Bed-Stuy. Above them, a three-by-three-foot painting shouts "marry me baby" in a saturated royal blue. It was how Jenna proposed to Mackenzie a little more than a year earlier: a command, not a question.

Jenna already knew that Mackenzie planned to marry her. "Mackenzie had been asking me to marry her every day, practically since we met. She'd just be like, 'You're gonna marry me,' just casually, all the time. And I would always be like, 'No' or 'I don't know' or 'whatever.'"

MACKENZIE: I relentlessly pursued her for years before she finally agreed to—

JENNA: Yeah, it was a bit hairy. I tried to shake her off for a while.

Mackenzie was persistent. It's possible that it's because, to her, they seemed inevitable. In August of 2017, Mackenzie had gone to a hypnotherapist to try to understand some of the dreams she'd been having—dreams that she said felt like memories from a past life. "I had been dealing with this one that felt like a memory of being left by somebody that I had never met before," she says. At the time, Mackenzie—also known as the indie musician Torres—was about to release her third album, and Jenna had already become a known figure painter in the States and in Europe. But their worlds had little crossover; they had no reason to know each other. That summer, Mackenzie walked out of St. Dymphna's bar in New York's East Village just as Jenna and a friend were walking in. "It was her."

Mackenzie had been at the bar with a friend—the same person that Jenna's friend was supposed to meet up with. So Mackenzie turned right around and followed the woman that had been in her dreams back into the bar.

That night, like so many queer origin stories before it, ended in a bar bathroom stall.

JENNA: We went inside and Mackenzie proceeded to buy everyone round after round of drinks. Things got a little sloppy. I think within the first hour, my legs were like draped over her lap. And then she followed me into the bathroom, and the rest is history. Sort of.

"Sort of" because Jenna did end up leaving Mackenzie—about a year into their relationship.

MACKENZIE: It was exactly like the memory that I had, only it turned out to not be a memory. It was, I guess, a premonition.

JENNA: I thought she was way too young. I'm twelve years older than Mackenzie. So when we met, I was like, "Oh, this will be fun to, like, make out with her or something." But I didn't really consider it as potentially serious.

When I ask how long it took her to change her mind, neither of them have a clear answer. Perhaps things shifted when they finally moved in together? Definitely by the time Jenna proposed. Whenever it happened, it was a product of Mackenzie's sheer persistence. She has a sort of guileless intensity that feels undeniable—even in the most mundane ways. At one point during their photo shoot for this book, she started talking about a Nashville hot chicken sandwich from a spot in their Brooklyn neighborhood that she *loved*. Every few minutes, the conversation would come back to this sandwich. She wasn't even trying to convince anyone to get the sandwich; she was just reveling in the memory of how much she loved it. By the time we were ordering lunch, I had never wanted a sandwich more. (We ordered four. They were great.) She seems to love Jenna in a similar way—consistently, intensely, and unselfconsciously.

It also comes out as a sort of gentle bluntness. Mackenzie was the first person to offer an edit to the framing that I presented to everyone in the book: that "queer power couples" were a relatively new phenomenon; that to be out, coupled, and allowed to influence mainstream culture had only really become possible in the last ten years. "I mean, I personally would say the last three to five."

MACKENZIE: I was raised in a really conservative Christian home in Macon, Georgia. So I didn't know any gay people. I didn't know *of* any gay or queer people at all, apart from Ellen and Rosie. And Elton John. And every time any of those people came up, one of my parents would be like, "They're very talented. However, we know that the lifestyle choice that they've made is sinful." So I never missed the fact that I wasn't allowed to be queer.

    I went to college in Nashville, Tennessee, which is relatively conservative, but not as conservative as Macon, Georgia. And I didn't date in college. I did a lot of, you know, getting drunk and making out with girls and then being like, "Oops." Which is hilarious, looking back. And then I moved to New York around the time that my first album came out, in 2013. And that was also when I got my first girlfriend, and I was like, "I guess this is it; this is what I'm doing!"

JENNA: You were out before that.

MACKENZIE: I think it was between 2012 and 2013 that I started to slowly come out to friends, and maybe I would allude to it on social media. I was never really explicit for a long time. A lot of that was just fear. I mean, even then, ten years ago, I was afraid. Obviously I was afraid of my parents and the whole community that I came from rejecting me. But I think even more so, afraid that the world would reject me, that I wouldn't be able to have the career that I wanted, on the level that I wanted. I was afraid of being a "niche" musician because I was gay. And I never wanted that to be the first thing that someone thought of when they thought of me. So I guess it was in that time that I just sort of embraced it.

    Around that time, I was very hurtfully outed to my parents. I didn't get to come out to them. But it was a blessing, honestly, because I think it would have taken me years. It was like a Band-Aid being ripped off. And that has been a really tense part of my life, but everything else is so much better for it.

Her queerness is "not really something that can be discussed between my parents and I," she says. I asked if anything changed after she told her parents she and Jenna were engaged—if that's something that they can perceive as "traditional."

MACKENZIE: You know, I told them, and—I mean, it's insane. My mom was like, "You are?" and that's kind of it. That's the last time it came up.

She assures me that she's okay, though: "I'm in therapy," she says with a smile. And it might help that Jenna's experience had a lot of parallels to hers.

JENNA: I'm also from the South. I grew up in Tennessee, in Knoxville, which is a little bigger than Macon, but it was [also] twelve years before Mackenzie. It's funny that she says Rosie and Ellen, because those were the only lesbians I ever knew of also. And it definitely hindered my ability to identify with my queerness. I also was raised Mormon, so it was kind of the double whammy of, like, the inability to conceive of queerness.

"Things just sort of revealed themselves over a long and painful process," Jenna says. She got married young, and was in relationships with men for a long time. But those relationships were open, and she often dated women. "When I would try to not see other people, I would really feel like I was missing something by not being with women. And then eventually, it became pretty clear."

JENNA: It took a really long time. I was much older than I think I would have been if circumstances had been different—if there had been more representation and I hadn't been raised in those particular cultural circumstances.

Jenna is now best known for her paintings of Mackenzie. When we go to her studio, we're greeted by two larger-than-life full-body portraits of her hanging on the walls—both of which have already been snagged by collectors. Some of her portraits are painted from her perspective while they're having sex. Others seem almost leering, putting a spotlight on a half-naked Mackenzie—or, like the piece titled *You Blinded by M*, letting that half-naked Mackenzie put a spotlight on you. Jenna pulls out a hot-pink tube of paint. "This is a very important color around here." It's the neon paint she always uses for Mackenzie's nipples. She jokes that it should be renamed Gribbon Nipple Pink.

JENNA: It's funny. When I met Mackenzie, she immediately entered my work. I was just painting her all the time. So the paintings, I guess, allowed me to come out without actually saying anything to anyone. Everything was there in the paintings.

  In spite of what it looks like, I'm a pretty private person. It takes a long time for me to want anyone outside of my close circle to know anything about my private life. So it was kind of nice to let the paintings do the work in that way. It was pretty clear. I was literally painting us having sex. So it was like every person that I had ever known kind of knew this through seeing my paintings. Even my parents.

I ask her if she ever considered *not* sharing the paintings publicly—did she ever consider hiding from that kind of visibility? Did they talk about it?

JENNA: I think it was inevitable. After you make like a hundred paintings of someone, it's like—

MACKENZIE: But before you made the hundred paintings.

JENNA: I made the paintings before there even could have been a conversation. From the very beginning of our relationship, I was painting her. It wasn't a conscious decision—I was just making the paintings I wanted to make.

And I was fixated on her. The work just sort of naturally follows the fixation. And she's such a good subject. She's so dynamic. She was just inspiring, with or without having an agenda. And then I was like, "Am I really going to put this painting out there?" And then that's when the question is answered with, "I have to put the painting out there." Because it might not have been the reason to make the painting, but it was a reason to share the painting with the world.

It was a strange feeling. And I did feel super exposed making those paintings. But just from having the experience of growing up without access to any kind of representation, it felt really important to put something out there that might make someone else's journey a little easier. And a little less, I don't know, blind?

When I talk to them in 2022, their most recent and most celebrated works are both about each other. Mackenzie's fifth album, *Thirstier*, wallows in the years when Jenna was still pulling away from her. (On the title track, she sings: "I'll admit that sometimes I'm afraid that you'll still run / Aim and shoot your arrow at a new obsession / But if I've got permission to stay under your skin / You'll never want another love as long as you live.")

It means that, for the majority of their relationship, they've invited other people to perceive them— both their relationship and how they see one another.

JENNA: People get so many things wrong. But when you put art out there, you don't get to dictate the way people consume it or what it's going to mean to them. And so we just kind of laughed sometimes about like—

MACKENZIE: —*how* wrong they are. People think that we're sisters.

JENNA: Especially in my work. It happens all the time. Or people think that my paintings are all self-portraits. And in fact, in one, there was one post from my most recent show in London, and it was all these paintings of Mackenzie, with our limbs entwined. You can see our bodies and our anatomy and whatever. And someone posted and was like, "These are paintings of the artist and her husband." I think she thought that Mackenzie was the artist and that the limbs belonged to a man. But, I mean, there was no indication that that was a man. People also think that I just paint self-portraits and that I'm her. I think I'm being so explicit and hitting people over the head with these ideas. And even then, people can't see it. Because they can't fathom that women are in relationships, romantically, together.

MACKENZIE: People can't wrap their heads around it. People can't believe that women are in relationships with each other.

JENNA: But I like that people can interpret it in a way that feels relevant to their own experience—which is clearly what's happening. That people use it as a way to mirror their own experiences and thoughts and ideas and project them onto us. Which is cool. But what really happens between us and what people think our relationship is could never be the same thing.

MACKENZIE: But what's hilarious about it, really, is that everything that we share is so calculated. I'm not actually giving away anything that I don't want to and neither is Jenna. We are the puppeteers here. It's part of being an artist and making things. And it's awesome that people see themselves in it, because that's ultimately what you want.

"Sisters" aside, both of their work is explicitly queer. With a twelve-year age difference between them, you'd think they would have grown up with vastly different access to queer culture—Mackenzie was in eighth grade when Facebook was invented, while Jenna was twenty-two when she first heard of Google. But they both grew up in really restrictive conservative environments—Mackenzie's was Baptist; Jenna's was Mormon—so they were almost equally isolated from any queer representation. Now they're very aware that they're creating the kind of representation that they didn't have in their conservative religious bubbles in Macon and Knoxville.

MACKENZIE: I think it's because I'm just singing from my own perspective. Most of the time when I'm writing songs, I feel kind of like a male country singer—like I'm Tim McGraw or Johnny Cash, and I'm just writin' about my girl. And it's never been an intentionally gendered thing. I'm just writing from my perspective, and it's my very honest perspective. And I think that just happens to be creating some representation for people like me.

Really, I'm just finally doing what I've always been inclined to do but was kind of afraid to early on. Obviously, there are a lot of people who have come before me who have paved the way, but I do feel, in this one pocket that I occupy, I'm doing a little bit.

So my priority is just being as real as possible. If I share something publicly that feels intense or really vulnerable, or a little negative, it's always just about being

FROM THE VERY BEGINNING OF OUR RELATIONSHIP, I WAS PAINTING HER. IT WASN'T A CONSCIOUS DECISION—I WAS JUST MAKING THE PAINTINGS I WANTED TO MAKE.

—*Jenna Gribbon*

the most real that I can. I'm not trying to make it look perfect. It's just sharing pieces of my life.

JENNA: It's kind of crazy because I lived the first almost forty years of my life with people having one idea about me, and then suddenly the narrative shifted. And it did feel very exposing. Being so public, you think about every person you've ever known and what they think about it. But I also kind of don't care what anybody thinks, you know? I'm just living my life, having my relationship, and making my work— just trying to be as true to my work and my love as I can be. And this is what it looks like.

But in the beginning, I felt very exposed. It's not really good or bad. It's just naked. And sometimes I want to delete my Instagram and not share anything else. Because sometimes it feels like too much. But then, I've had so many young girls and women who follow me send me messages about how meaningful the work is to them. And it makes me feel like I have to keep sharing.

Sometimes I feel like, who am I to have this position? I'm in a position I never expected to be in. I never thought that I was going to be a person who people would look to for queer representation, obviously. But it seems to be touching some people and making them feel seen or inspired or represented.

I ask if they remember the first person they recognized as queer. Mackenzie says Miss Honey, the famously queer-coded teacher from *Matilda*, without skipping a beat. Jenna is a little more hesitant.

JENNA: I never had any celebrity crushes growing up—not a single one. Maybe because of the queerness or maybe it just wasn't for me. Like, none of what's being sold to me is doing it for me.

But I was always really into these Victorian books about Victorian girls. I just wanted to be in that world and think about these Victorian girls. And it still kind of does it for me, like costume dramas—

MACKENZIE: She'll still watch a movie with Victorian girls having queer tension. And that will be what does it for her. Like, in nightgowns.

JENNA: Corsets, nightgowns, all those things. It's sort of all in that vein—Anne of Green Gables was probably, like, The Crush.

We joke about this all the time, because when I was a kid, I came home from school and I watched *Pollyanna* every single day after school. I was so obsessed with it as a little kid. And Mackenzie has a little bit of this Hayley Mills thing about her. And so there were all of these things that kind of aligned when I met Mackenzie.

I was like, "Oh, you're like this weird combination of every archetype I've ever been attracted to."

I actually made a whole series of paintings about projecting a kind of eroticism or romanticism onto fictional characters or cultural figures where it wasn't intended and I painted my friends as these characters. And it was about being able to do that—or about *having* to, because there's no representation of us in the culture, so we're just projecting it onto these characters that weren't intended to play that role.

Their doorbell rings, and Jenna's eleven-year-old son, Silas, comes barreling into the room with one of his friends. When she met Mackenzie, Jenna was in an open relationship with her partner, Julian Tepper, a novelist, musician, and Silas's dad. Now Silas splits his time between Julian's and Jenna and Mackenzie's homes. Mackenzie sweetly documents their family outings—buying a Christmas tree, going to gallery openings, voting—on social media.

Silas's voice echoes through the hallways as he and his friend disappear down the stairs, and the room is quiet again. Jenna and Mackenzie's living room is a glaring combination of the two of them—fine art all over the walls and guitar stands blocking off the fireplace. There's one wall lined with Mackenzie's cowboy boots, and another with Jenna's collection of monochrome oxfords. (It was also the room where Jenna gave Mackenzie a stick-and-poke tattoo of a lavender sprig during our photo shoot.) Their basement used to be Jenna's studio, but now it's Mackenzie's rehearsal space—an almost perfect recreation of the East Village apartment she lived in when they met ("where I was generally stoned twenty-four seven").

They share in each other's work whenever possible. Jenna's been in several of Mackenzie's music videos; she even made one of them. And when she's not on tour, Mackenzie helps Jenna in her studio, organizing paints and prepping canvases.

MACKENZIE: I've learned from her how to hold myself accountable to the work—treating the art like a nine-to-five—which I wasn't as good at, at all. In the East Village, I was getting stoned all day. Things are a lot better in that way now.

She's really softened me up too. I feel like my heart, it's just so mushy now. Which is unfortunate because I have no defenses anymore. I cry all the time now. But I had to open up if I wanted to win her, basically. And I did the work, you know? I started going to therapy, and I've done a lot of work on myself. But as a result, I'm a better person. And that means I'm, you know, a little more weepy and vulnerable now.

JENNA: I learn from Mackenzie all the time—how to stand up for myself and be more brave in that way. I think I'm brave in a lot of ways. I'm brave about going after

TOP IMAGE:
Mackenzie,
photographed by
Jenna.

BOTTOM IMAGE:
Jenna,
photographed by
Mackenzie.

what I want. But I'm not brave about standing up for myself in ways that are really important. And she's helped me be more brave in that way.

MACKENZIE: That's so nice, baby.

They punctuate most sentences to each other with *baby*. And it's not a quick term of endearment—they seem to luxuriate in it, like it's a treat to be able to say it to each other every time.

It's part of why it's so fitting that the painting on their wall yells, "marry me baby."

After waiting out the Covid lockdowns, they got married in November of 2022. The ceremony was officiated by musician Sarah Jaffe, and everyone was in impeccable broad-shouldered suiting, including Silas.

But when I first interviewed them earlier that year, Jenna was still keeping up the act.

MACKENZIE: I didn't really think she was ever gonna follow through on something like a marriage.

JENNA: I'm a little slippery. And it hasn't happened yet. It's happening . . .

MACKENZIE: It's happening.

JENNA: We'll see.

BARBARA BELMONT

(SHE/HER)
CHEMIST

ROCHELLE "SHELLEY" DIAMOND

(SHE/HER)
RESEARCH
BIOLOGIST

THE FIRST QUESTION BARBARA ASKS ME when we start our interview is "Why us?"

We are on a video call—the two of them dialing in from separate rooms in their Craftsman house in Pasadena, with nearly identical glasses and even more identical headsets. "Yeah, how did you find us?" Shelley says. "We're not like Buttigieg or Ellen or Portia."

I chuckle a bit but quickly realize they actually want an answer. I start with their résumés: Barbara Belmont is an analytical chemist and a lecturer at California State University, Dominguez Hills, and, in her words, a professional "chemical detective." Rochelle "Shelley" Diamond is a research biologist and the director of California Institute of Technology's Flow Cytometry and Cell Sorting Facility; she was on the team that first cloned synthetic human insulin.

But perhaps the top line of that CV is their activism. Together, in the early 1980s, they helped found the National Organization of Gay and Lesbian Scientists and Technical Professionals—the first professional society for LGBTQ people in STEM. (They recognize that sentence is a bit of an "alphabet soup.") They were the first scientific organization to nationally call out the Reagan administration for the lack of research funding during the AIDS crisis. "We were the professional group opposite ACT UP," Shelley says. And when the male co-chairs died of complications from AIDS, "we picked up the reins." Now they fund scholarships for queer people in STEM, run summits, and teach scientific organizations how to build LGBTQ-inclusion programs. Their mandate, put simply, is to combat homophobia in STEM.

They seem satisfied by my answer, so I ask them the question I start nearly every interview with: How did they meet?

Ironically—given their mandate—it was a homophobic engineer who brought them together.

In 1978, Shelley was working in a lab that was trying to build a gas-phase protein sequencer—a tool that helps scientists understand diversity in cells—when an engineer from the "biomedical instrumentation division" was assigned to the project.

SHELLEY: It turned out that he was extremely homophobic. At the time, I was married to a man—he was my best friend, and he knew my proclivities. I was having an affair, and this engineer found out and started sabotaging my instrument. And it was really tough. And I was finally asked to leave because I wasn't getting anywhere. So I left; I went to UCLA. Another infamous project, for it was the first time gene therapy was going to be tried. And during that time, my husband called me up and said, "I know why you were canned. The engineer went out and had lunch with all of us and had too many martinis and told everybody how he ran you out of the department."

At the time, I was having this affair. On a Saturday morning, my lover and I were lying in her bed, and we were listening to a National Public Radio program called *I Am, Are You?* And a woman by the name of Amy Ross was talking about Los Angeles Gay and Lesbian Scientists and telling about how they were meeting. And so my lover dared me to go. And I went to Los Angeles Gay and Lesbian Scientists, and I met Amy Ross. And I don't know how long later Barbara came along to one of those meetings . . .

BARBARA: A year later. I didn't know anybody like me. I had also been married to a man and I left him for a woman—another scientist—who turned out to be, you know, an immature, self-centered nine-year-old. She was the center of the world as far as she saw it. And I didn't know any other scientists.

So as I was coming out, I did the thing that women in my generation at that time could do to meet other women—went to rap groups. And these were like lesbian, feminist, separatist rap groups. Not the music.

We got into some pretty heated arguments about science and the role of science. And that was an identity I was really wrapped up into, and here I was around all these people who are saying, "No, no, that's part of the patriarchy. That's terrible." And I'm like, "Huh. I don't know if I want to be friends with you people." So I didn't know where to look. There wasn't internet, and I am not a drinker or a smoker. And so I just couldn't go to bars to meet people.

But I saw a letter to the editor in *Science* magazine, sort of a declaration of existence of an organization called National Organization of Gay and Lesbian Scientists. And I went, "Ah, my people!" I wrote them a letter, and the letter bounced because they had listed the PO box wrong. So maybe a year later, I got my hands on the gay Yellow Pages from the local lesbian bookstore, and I started looking through it, because, you know, I'm that kind of nerd: I look through things and I read and read and read. I learned that there were all these organizations for everything, like, you know, bicyclists and photographers. And I found this Los Angeles Gay and Lesbian Scientists club. And so I wrote to them. And it turned out they had just recently started these Sunday women's potlucks, and I got up my gumption to go.

I was not looking for a partner in any way. I was partnered—even though in retrospect, I can see that was a huge mistake. I was just looking for other people like me—people who enjoyed science, nerds. People who were interested in things and how things worked. And so I went to this potluck event. And that was where I met Shelley.

Shelley and I wound up being on a committee together for the women's program, and we were hanging out a lot.

SHELLEY: We were in charge of events, and we had to go check out each site for the event, right? Which meant, "Oh, let's go to the tide pools." So we would go to the tide pools.

BARBARA: One step led to a kiss. And then it was all over. We were in love with each other about a year later.

But we reconcile our anniversary to the 1983 confession we gave to each other that we were in love. And I said it first.

SHELLEY: We were at her work—

BARBARA: —at Caltech.

SHELLEY: She showed me the location where their new lab was going to be. And I don't know what—we were probably making out. And then she was looking at my eyes and said, "Are my eyes telling you that I'm in love with you?"

BARBARA: And she said—you're not going to believe this—she said, "I was afraid of that."

Shelley was in love with her too, but like most things, it wasn't that simple. Throughout our conversations, Shelley often refers to her "entanglements"—a product, it seems, of having to spend a decade in the closet.

SHELLEY: I grew up in Phoenix, Arizona. And my family were very prominent socially. My family owned a chain of department stores. It's now [part of] Dillard's, but it used to be called Diamond's. And I had two older brothers, much older brothers. And I was the only girl in my generation.

She never quite fit into the society set, she says.

SHELLEY: I was a tomboy. I had my Lone Ranger Six Guns. I had my hobby horse. My cousins had horses, and I used to ride them. I played softball; I played football with the guys.

I was in love with my next-door neighbor—a girl whose parents owned the Chevrolet dealership. And when my brothers got married, I fell in love with my youngest brother's wife. I was a young girl, but I loved sitting next to her on long car trips and putting my head on her breast.

Then I turned sixteen and I was expected to have a real coming-out.

This is the only interview in this book where "coming out" refers to anything other than coming out of the closet.

SHELLEY: I had to take cotillion. I had to learn how to curtsy for the queen; I had to learn how to pour the tea for the queen. I had to learn how to dance with boys and lead them going backward.

BARBARA: Which she still can do.

SHELLEY: I asked my best friend, Cliff, if he would take me. Cliff lived "across the tracks." He borrowed his father's car, which was a Chevy Malibu convertible. He went to Pep Boys, and he bought a seat belt that went from the passenger seat to the driver's seat so that I could sit next to him.

But the evening didn't go to plan—at all. Shelley had thought she'd had the flu a couple weeks earlier, but it turned out to be viral encephalitis, a dangerous brain infection. She passed out in the bathroom, was taken to the hospital, and spent the next year and a half making a slow, difficult recovery. "It was only in my senior year of high school that I was able to walk around on my own," she says. She got out of a wheelchair just in time to go to college, which made it feel all the more important.

SHELLEY: I wanted to go to UC Berkeley, like my brothers did. But my parents sent me to a finishing school in Denver—all women—and the idea was that I should get my MRS. [author's note: "Getting your MRS degree" was a slang term for going to college to find a husband.]

Every weekend, on Saturday morning, the bus would drive around, and everybody would get on and go to the Air Force Academy to the dances or to the Colorado School of Mines to their dances. And you were expected to date.

But I also saw, for my very first time, a lesbian couple at the end of the hall. And I was like, "Ding!" Because I was falling in love with all my friends, my roommates, my suitemates.

But on the very first day of orientation, there was an announcement that if you were caught as a lesbian, you would be automatically expelled. And I had to ask somebody what "lesbian" was.

BARBARA: What did they say?

SHELLEY: That's when two girls love each other. I had never heard of that.

BARBARA: You didn't even have the vocabulary.

SHELLEY: I didn't have the vocabulary. I just knew I wanted to be one of them.

BARBARA: I definitely had the vocabulary because my husband and I enjoyed reading *Penthouse Letters*. So I had the vocabulary—not in grade school or high school, but I definitely had it by the time I was eighteen. We were a seventies couple. I developed quite a vocabulary.

SHELLEY: When my brothers would come home from college—maybe I was seven, eight, or nine—they would have *Playboy* under their beds. And I would steal them.

BARBARA: You liked to look at the ladies?

SHELLEY: Yep. But there wasn't any dialogue with it. There wasn't anything like your *Penthouse* thing.

BARBARA: Oh, no, that's why *Penthouse* was superior.

Barbara knew she loved women at least a decade before *Penthouse* came into her life.

BARBARA: I can remember being six or seven and having a big crush on a ten-year-old girl in my grade school. But the only role model I had was my mother's cousin, who was stone butch.

Then our babysitter's daughter—I messed around with her. I must have been six or seven years old. And she's about the same age. And then I found out that she was committed to an institution because she was messing around with girls. And that was scary.

It was in the sixties, so I think I was really lucky to be an adolescent in the seventies. I still knew I loved women. And there was a lot of openness and tolerance about free love and all that, so I didn't hear as much homophobia. And so I was very openly interested in women. But I also was interested in men. So I didn't date any women. I honestly think I didn't really wake up, like, hormonally or sexually until I was about nineteen. And then that desire to be with a woman was just overwhelming.

I consider my coming-out to be the first time I was intimate with a woman. I was essentially sitting on the fence. And that pushed me over. We were just watching *A League of Their Own* [the extremely queer 2022 television adaptation], and the catcher said, "Well, you know, with men, it's nice. It's like warm bread with butter on it. But, you know, with women, it's just like, 'Wow.'" [author's note: More explicitly, Abbi Jacobson's character compared having sex with women to pizza. Which, well, fair.] I could really relate to what the catcher was saying.

I fell in love with somebody while I was still married to my husband. And the vision I had had when I married him was, "Well, I like women. Maybe I'll find some other housewife—some lady in the PTA, when I've got my kids in school. Maybe I'll find somebody like me, and we can have a thing on the side." I was perfectly happy with that idea. But then after I fell in love with this woman, that didn't work out.

And then I met somebody else, and we fell in love. And then I just couldn't. I couldn't even stay home. And wound up leaving around 1980. And, you know, that was well and good for a few months. And then it turned out that she really wasn't the right person for me, but she was definitely the right person to get me out of that relationship and get me on course for, you know, being the lesbian that I am.

Meanwhile, Shelley was also going through the motions of marrying a man: Cliff, in fact, the boy who took her to cotillion.

SHELLEY: He got sick—Crohn's disease—and he needed insurance. So I put him on my insurance, and we got married. I figured, "Well, he's my best friend. I might as well marry him and take care of him."

BARBARA: When did you start seeing other women?

SHELLEY: At City of Hope—that's where I met Leisha.

BARBARA: So my question is, how did you know and how did she signal that something could happen?

SHELLEY: She asked about me. She came and she helped me with some things in the lab. And she kept probing and probing, and I said, "Well, I'm kind of AC/DC—going both ways, bisexual."

BARBARA: That was the seventies term for *bi*.

SHELLEY: And then she says, "So have you ever kissed a woman?" I said no. And she said, "Well, come out to the parking lot."
  And so one thing led to another, and she came over and kissed me on our couch. And we made out, and that was first time I was with a woman, and my head blew off. Absolutely blew off. I was absolutely smitten.
  And then I found out she had another lover.

BARBARA: Oops.

SHELLEY: That had been her lover all along. I had no idea.
  So then I stopped seeing Leisha, because she had Pauline. And I wanted the best for her. And then I started going to the women's bar in Pasadena. And one of the people who played almost every Saturday night was Melissa Etheridge—I used to buy her drinks. And I started playing on the bar's softball team. I was a catcher.

And so I dated a couple of women on the team. And then I met a woman at the bar who I liked. She was Mexican American, and I moved into her trailer with her. And then we moved to the house with Cliff.

That's about the time I met Barbara. And I would wait for Cliff to go to sleep and then stand by the phone for hours hoping Barbara would call.

BARBARA: Because, you know, landlines.

SHELLEY: Sordid history.

The "entanglements" didn't quite end there.

BARBARA: It took about maybe four years to realize that we wanted to be exclusive and committed with each other. And in that four-year gap, there was a lot of messy, messy relationship changes and terminations and stuff.

Self-portrait taken by Barbara and Shelley.

SHELLEY: We ended up deciding to live with a bunch of women scientists, all together, including people that we were dating or people who we're entangled with, and we tried that for about three years.

But then I got a divorce, and I had money to buy a house, and I decided that I was monogamous. I didn't like being with more than one person at a time. It was driving me nuts. So I bought a house, and I asked her to come with me.

BARBARA: And I came.

Shelley's family wasn't along for this ride. Her parents passed away before she was able to come out to them, but she did get to come out to "the matriarch of the family," Aunt Rose. Barbara, on the other hand, pulled her family into the fold.

BARBARA: When I decided to divorce my husband, I felt it was really, really important for my family to know the reason why. He was a very good person, and I didn't want them to think for a minute that he had caused this divorce. So the news of the divorce came with the news of the reason, which was that I was leaving him for another woman and that I was gay.

We made an appointment with my mom to go over and tell her about it. And she's like, "Oh, so what's the news you have for me?" And I said, "Well, we're getting a divorce." She goes, "Why?" "Because I love women." And she's like, "Oh, well, I knew that." She thought we were coming to tell her that we were pregnant. So she was disappointed in that. But her reaction by the end of the conversation was, "How can I help you with this process?" So I asked her to let the immediate family know.

My grandmother was a little bit upset for about twenty-four hours and then got to thinking, "I love my granddaughter. She's my first granddaughter, and I love her so much. And she's actually not any different now. I just know this thing about her that I didn't know before." And so, within twenty-four hours, she was on board. And if Grandma was on board, everybody's happy.

They still live in the same house that Shelley bought them in 1987, in a Pasadena neighborhood called "Bungalow Heaven." When you walk into their house, to your right you'll find a blanket from the American Chemical Society, woven with the periodic table of the elements, and to your left is a baby grand piano. After spending a few hours with them, they finally let it slip that they both compose, and with a mischievous smile, Barbara wiggled her fingers and began to play.

After almost forty years, their home is rich with their shared history. They got married just two miles away from the house, and they're Aunt Shelley and Barbie to their beloved grandnieces. Shelley is known for her pies. (The trick is painting the top of the crust with heavy cream, she says. "That's what you get when you put a chemist and a biologist in a kitchen.") And her cookies get some attention too.

The professional group they helped start—the National Organization for Gay and Lesbian Scientists and Technical Professionals—is now called Out to Innovate. "We wanted to make sure that all queers know they are welcome to be a part of the organization," Barbara explains.

The organization has evolved with the needs of the community. In the '80s, it was the AIDS crisis. "People were dying," Shelley says. "And ACT UP's work drove the scientific community to us. And we were able to put up programming in the scientific community to discuss these things."

But as the decades went on, their programming grew with the times. You can see it in the titles of their workshops: In 1994, the most outdated, there was "Social, Ethical, and Scientific Perspectives of Biological Research on Sexual Orientation"; in 2014, there was "LGBTQ and Allies in STEM: Mentoring and Resources"; and finally, in 2016, they offered "Bringing Your Whole LGBTQIQ Self to Work and School."

Today, on their website, they're careful to acknowledge that homophobia is still a part of their field. (Of their members, they say, "Those of us who are able are out and proud.") But they encourage those who can to embrace visibility in the field. Their project 500 Queer Scientists crowdsourced profiles of LGBTQ+ people in STEM (alphabet soup again). As of 2023, the project has collected more than 1,700 stories.

Their work, at its core, is making sure that queer scientists can find community—and can look around and see people like them. "We want to make sure that people don't have the same crisis I had," Barbara says, "wondering where everybody else was."

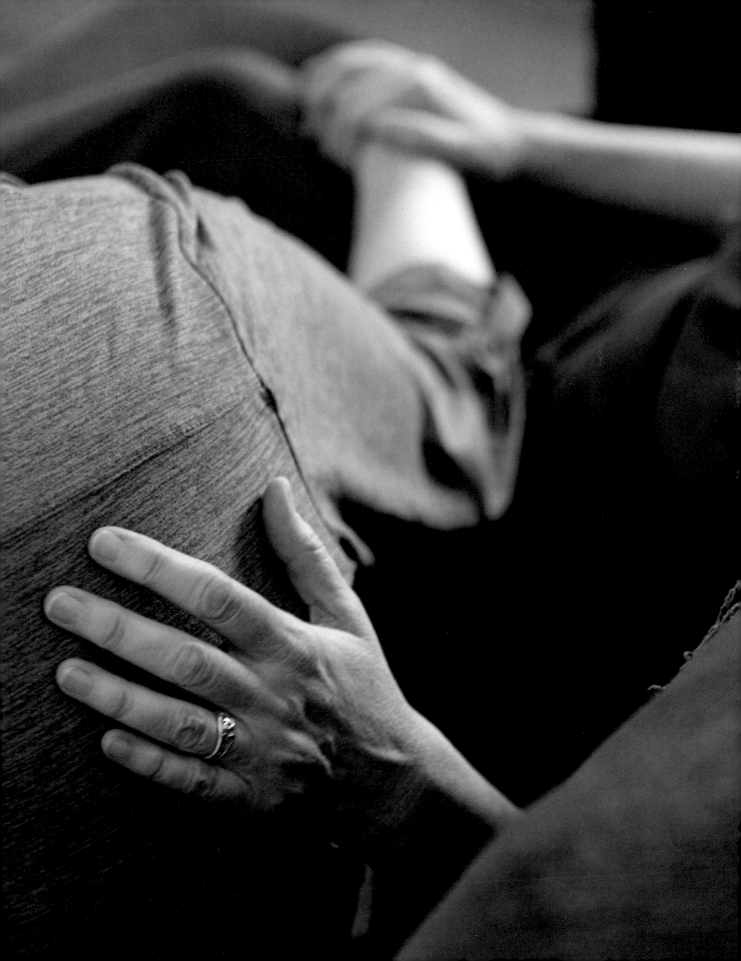

CANDY FEIT

(SHE/HER)
PHOTOGRAPHER

LYDIA POLGREEN

(SHE/HER)
JOURNALIST

IN 2004, LYDIA POLGREEN WAS OFFERED A DREAM JOB for a young journalist: foreign correspondent for the *New York Times* in their West Africa bureau. Her wife, Candy Feit, was a photographer, so she could work from anywhere. They were set.

The one hiccup: The bureau was based in Senegal, where homosexuality was punishable by up to five years in jail. Nearly twenty years later, talking to them in their Connecticut summer home, I ask them how they prepared for that. They were both surprised by how little they'd considered it. "At the time, I was just like, 'It's gonna be an adventure!'" Lydia says. "I was so heedless about it—so excited about being a foreign correspondent."

She wonders if maybe Candy was more worried at the time than she let on—but didn't want to dampen Lydia's enthusiasm. "Maybe? But I was also like, 'It's not a thing that we're *not* going to do. This is Lydia's dream.'"

That one decision would eventually bring them around the world, but it would also force them to constantly consider their own visibility for the next decade. The first alarm went off when Lydia went to visit the bureau.

CANDY: I remember you were talking to a photographer, and there was this guy, Joe, who worked for the *New York Times* for like ten years. He's sort of the house manager—he had this very amorphous role in the lives of the correspondents. And this guy was like, "Oh, Joe's gonna have an issue with you guys together." I think I was in denial until I was in situations, logistically, where I was like, "Oh, this is not normal. This is actually not how other people are living."

Lydia and Candy lived abroad for ten years, first in Senegal, then India, and finally in South Africa. And in between, Lydia won a Polk Award for her coverage of the war in Darfur. But they've been back in the States for the last ten years now. Since coming back, Lydia has been the editor in chief of the *Huffington Post* and the head of content at Gimlet Media before coming full circle and returning to the *New York Times* in a prestigious role as an opinion columnist.

Candy worked as a photojournalist in West Africa and India but soon realized that her heart was in documentary photography. She went on to capture queer subcultures across the world—from India's Kothi to Brooklyn's queer kink community. Most recently, though, she took a sharp left turn and went back to school to get her master's in social work. When we met them in their Fort Greene apartment, they'd just thrown a huge graduation party. The highlight: a shrimp luge. (Google it. Trust me.)

Their decade abroad still seems to form some of the contours of their world. You can see it in their home: At the front door, you're greeted by a massive wooden statue from Senegal; a beautiful glass

cabinet holds their bar—a find from South Africa; and a table in their living room is filled exclusively with trinkets, including a three-legged pig from Mexico.

They speak about that decade now with the wisdom of retrospect.

CANDY: I think when we went into living overseas—even though both of us had been completely out in our work environment and out to all of our friends and our families—it still felt acceptable [to not be out] in certain circumstances. It just wasn't convenient or prudent or safe to be out. And I think that's the thing that's definitely changed. We're in our mid-forties, so I'd be very curious what a *New York Times* correspondent who is going to be in West Africa—who's queer, who's in their late twenties, as we were then—how would they handle it? Would they see that as okay to sort of keep it secret? And it's funny—I think the fact that we were two women living together probably did not seem as strange, because we're living in cultures where—

LYDIA: Everyone thought we were twins. No, it's funny. People think we're sisters, we're twins. Which is really weird. But we were living in cultures where two women living together

WE HAD BOTH THE BURDEN OF BEING OUTSIDERS BUT ALSO THE PRIVILEGE OF BEING OUTSIDERS.... WE WERE IN THIS POLITE-SOCIETY SITUATION WHERE WE COULD LIVE OUR LIVES RELATIVELY NORMALLY, BUT YOU KNOW THAT YOU'RE LIVING IN A SOCIETY THAT TREATS QUEER PEOPLE REALLY, REALLY BADLY.

—*Lydia Polgreen*

and spending all their time together is actually not that unusual. The fact that we weren't married to men was probably the most unusual thing.

Everywhere that we went, I think we had both the burden of being outsiders but also the privilege of being outsiders. We were operating in societies that had these deeply, deeply homophobic cultures, which are absolutely colonial—homophobia was a colonial import to much of Africa. The British brought it; the French brought it. And the same is true in India. Because we were outsiders—we were able to kind of float above, and if people had suspicions or concerns, they would keep them to themselves.

But I actually covered stories of queer people who faced very, very real danger. We were living in West Africa at a time when there was this huge panic over homosexuality. And in Nigeria and Uganda and all of these countries, there were governments that were trying to pass laws that would impose the death penalty for homosexuality. So it is this weird dissonance: We were in this polite-society situation where we could live our lives relatively normally, but you know that you're living in a society that treats queer people really, really badly.

At the same time, Candy was also covering those communities—like her series on India's Kothi community—in extremely intimate settings.

CANDY: I never went into those situations super out. But of course, everyone knew I was gay. I never really discussed my personal life until like trip number two. Then people would start to ask me questions like "Who's the man?" or "Who's the top?" All those questions. "Are you having sex?" All a little bit personal. But also, at that point, what is personal between people? You're in their place. You're watching them undress. You're talking to them about their deep childhood traumas. So if someone's like, "Are you a top or a bottom?" I can't be like, "Oh, my God, I could never answer that." So at a certain point, I was like, "Okay, this is how lesbians work. And this is how I work." And I could just kind of joke more about that and be more personal with it.

There are still moments that seem to stick in both of their minds—moments where they feel weird about how much they concealed about themselves or accommodated other people's discomfort.

CANDY: Many years after we were in Africa, we were in India, and I was with a journalist who's a good friend, and we were doing a story for the *Globe and Mail*, and we were interviewing a guy. And he said, "Oh, what does your husband do?" And I was like, "Oh, he works for the *New York Times*." And then he was like, "Oh, is your husband Jim Yardley?" He was the other correspondent in India at that time. I was like, "Yeah. My husband is Jim Yardley."

And we know that queer people exist in all cultures, right? In all cultures and all places, throughout time. And so there is a sense you can pick up—I don't think it's quite on a conscious level—how to act where you are, right? And vice versa. People know when they see us or when they see us interact, or when they're in our home. But unless you are like, "Hello, I'm gay. This is my wife, we're together, we have sex, we sleep in the same bed," I think there is some way that people accommodate one another.

LYDIA: Yeah, but it's an accommodation through silence. And that's the thing that you realize. I think for us, when we were living in India, and were moving to South Africa, I think one thing that was a really big relief was like, okay, in going to South Africa, we're going to a country that actually has greater constitutional protections, at that time, for queer people than the United States does. But I think for us, in some ways, as a couple, we just assumed that this was the thing; we were gonna have to figure out a way to navigate the world. And know when it was okay and know when it was not okay.

And I think it's very much a generational thing—growing up the way that both of us did in society, in families where queerness was invisible and no one ever really talked about it. It was actually really easy to slip back into that mode of code-switching. Like, these are the spaces where it's okay to be who you are. And these are the spaces where it's not.

That kind of accommodation traces back to where they met—St. John's College. "Whenever we say, 'Oh, we met in college,'" Candy says, "it's like, 'No, no, no, not a normal college. Like, a weird place.'"

LYDIA: We went to this tiny, tiny little college that did not have a lot of queer people in it—or not a lot of visible queer people in it. And actually was, in a weird way, a pretty conservative place. And I think we both ended up there through these very strange journeys. My father had gone to this college and I hadn't taken the SAT because I was living overseas. And it was one of the few schools that didn't require the SAT to apply for admission. And I didn't want to wait for another year.

CANDY: I really did not love my family-of-origin living situation in high school. And I could go there early, so I left high school and started my freshman year basically six months early. It meant I was kind of shifted a year ahead, but it also meant I didn't have to be with my family and I could go and start my life. Come to find out it is a hotbed of crazy conservatives. One of the members of my graduating class was Mitch McConnell's chief of staff. And by the way, we graduated with like seventy-five people. So these are people that we really know. And then one guy wrote an op-ed [in support of] Amy Coney Barrett in the *Washington Post*.

It wound up being a really difficult experience for me. In ways I didn't realize until quite a while after. And I almost feel a little bit ashamed that I wasn't aware of the impact it had on me when I was there. Like Lydia said, there weren't any queer people, there wasn't any visual arts—

LYDIA: Very few people of color.

CANDY: Very few people of color.

LYDIA: It's funny because I think we both ended up at this school because we wanted to get away from where we were. And it's kind of extraordinary that, in that place, we found each other. And we literally have been together ever since. We've been together since 1996. And we've known each other since 1994.

It's funny because it was a very college thing, you know? We were both really smitten with each other. Candy wore these overalls and was really into the Dave Matthews Band.

CANDY: Both true. Both totally true. I liked other things too. I didn't only like Dave Matthews.

LYDIA: She grew sprouts on a windowsill of her dorm room. It was a very nineties situation. She wore Birkenstocks, as did I.

CANDY: And now they're back!

In that environment, neither of them actively hid their queerness, but they also didn't rush to come out.

LYDIA: I was a very serious student—very nerdy. And I think we were both really into each other, but also not really out? But not really in the closet either?

CANDY: I mean, I was wearing overalls and Birkenstocks.

LYDIA: [*laughing*] Transmitting it to the world! I think that I was not out when we met, but I think I was by the time we were actually dating.

CANDY: Lydia came out, officially, in school. The idea of coming out is so complicated, but I was kind of out but not. I wasn't in; I wasn't out. In 2021, if you behave like I behaved, no one would be like, "Are you gay? Are you queer? What's your deal?" Because it would be so obvious. But then it wasn't a thing that people assumed. I was out in ninety-six. But very slowly.

LYDIA: Late bloomer.

Before St. John's, Lydia had grown up in Kenya and Ghana, both countries that outlaw homosexuality. "At my high school [in Ghana]," she says, "I wrote an op-ed for the school paper, and at this time—and I definitely was not out in any way—but I remember having a reason to write an opinion piece about how gay people should be allowed to live or something like that. And even *that* being controversial." But her coming-out process, she says, was more informed by her parents' experiences than the environment she grew up in.

LYDIA: My mother is from Ethiopia. And when she was in her late teens, she was living in Addis Ababa and she had a boyfriend who was gay; she was his beard, basically. And she didn't really know that that was happening. People would talk about him, and finally, one day, she decided to ask him about it, and he beat her. She was devastated.

My father had grown up in a family where his brother was gay, and it was not great. But there was no violence associated with it. And so when I came out, my father was like, "Okay," but my mom thought this would lead to devastating consequences for me.

I think it's interesting. These were *their* experiences of queer love, but they were imprinted on me.

Her uncle was the first person Lydia ever recognized as queer—and he's remained a model for queer love ever since.

LYDIA: He and his husband took me and my brothers to Disney World. Well, they weren't husbands. Nobody explained exactly what they were. But they had been together since

Lydia, photographed by Candy.

Photograph of their home, by Lydia and Candy.

Self-portrait by Lydia and Candy.

I could remember. And they took us to Disney World. And it never occurred to me as a child to question what their relationship was. But when they were driving the car at one point, Mel put his hand on my uncle Tom's knee. And I was like, "Oh, oh!"

CANDY: That's awesome. I didn't know that. I mean, I knew about the trip . . .

LYDIA: Yeah!

CANDY: And they're still together!

LYDIA: I feel very lucky to have had my uncle as this role model of what it is to be a person who's out in every aspect of your life and uncompromising in expecting that your family, the people you work with, and that everybody is accepting of your whole self.

CANDY: My parents have this best friend who is a raging homophobe and racist. And he would talk about his cousin who is gay. And I was so fascinated by listening to him talk about her. My ears would kind of perk up, even when I was like ten. He only had negative things to say about her. But the first queer person I really clocked was this woman. When I was a teenager, I went to this summer program, and I met this older person—who was only twenty, and I was like fifteen or sixteen—and she was gay. She was super out, and I was like, "Oh, my God, what is it like to be you?" I was so enamored. It was just captivating. I was like, "Oh, wow. I like this. I feel like I get this. Something about this makes me feel things." And that was that. But I don't remember it being a "ring of keys" kind of thing. But I was always sort of—my ears would perk up.

When I started to come out to myself, I read all of the books—which were like five; it was the nineties—*Rubyfruit Jungle*, all of Sarah Schulman's books. So many of those books were kinda schlocky—not Sarah's books, but books like *Rubyfruit Jungle*. They were like girl meets girl, girl breaks girl's heart, girl's lonely. So I don't think I really had a role model of queer love.

My parents were married for a really long time, though. So I had a real blueprint for long-lasting marriages. But I think more as I matured—and went through therapy—I think yes, in some ways, I think my parents really were in love, and I think somehow they made it work. And they liked each other as much as they could like anybody and tolerated each other as much as they could tolerate anybody. But I always thought, "Oh, this is what people do. You meet your person and then you make it work."

I don't feel like it was so hard with you. I don't feel like we have to work at it—"Oh, gotta make it work for the dogs, can't break up."

Their life now is joyously queer. They spend two weeks in Provincetown every August. (Candy can usually be found in a colorful kaftan; Lydia, in impeccably cut suiting.) And in 2017, Lydia was named one of *Out* magazine's Out100. I ask them what the transition was like when they first came back to the States.

LYDIA: It was a really big change, right? Because I felt much freer to dress differently. It was okay to be more masculine presenting, and that wouldn't be a *thing*. I felt like you could just live your life. And no one really cared.

CANDY: The clothes thing, especially in India, was very much a thing. Of course the climate is a huge factor in it. But even if the cut of the clothes are kind of like roomy and a little bit androgynous, perhaps, you go in and you try to buy, like, a woman's kurta and it's, like, fucking flowers. It's very hyperfeminine. Because things are cut both the same for men and women. When we dressed up, we went to a few weddings, and we both wore saris, and, yeah, I think I know how you felt about that.

LYDIA: It felt weird. It definitely felt weird.

And it was a big relief, but at the same time, we had these extraordinary adventures, and, I think, in weird ways, being two women enabled us to be together in a lot of those adventures in ways that might have been harder if we were an opposite-sex couple or if we were two men. I think in most places—and I certainly felt this as a woman doing journalism—women were assumed not to be very important. And so constantly being underestimated meant that people would say things and do things in front of you that they probably wouldn't do if you're in front of a white man who was a journalist. So it was kind of a mixed bag.

Lydia's jobs have become more public-facing by the year, and it's allowed her to keep reevaluating what that kind of visibility means to her.

LYDIA: Over the course of my life, as I've been through a really interesting transition from being someone who primarily was focused on my own work—I was a reporter and a correspondent and wrote stories—and I think it was pretty easy for me in that work to be like, "I'm just a byline. My personality doesn't matter." And as I've stepped into more leadership positions, I think I've really questioned that perspective. It's become clear that it's really, really important that people who hold positions of power and are queer—or are Black or are nonbinary or whatever they are—hold that space and be visible and talk about it and be a role model for people and be like, "This is possible." You can have power and you can shape the culture—you can shape the world. And there are people like us who are doing that. As a younger person, I sort of thought that it's really just about me being able to do the work that I want to do. But as I've gotten older, it's become really clear that it's much more about making the path for other people to be able to do the things that I did when I was younger. And the things that I'm doing now.

CANDY: I don't really feel like I'm in the public eye. I'm just Lydia's plus-one. But because Lydia has a public-facing job, and because we are queer, it has given us access to a lot of beautiful experiences that I don't know I would have had if you didn't have a public job. Like Sarah Schulman—whose books I read at sixteen under the covers—is now our friend. To me that's incredible. I never thought I would one day be friends with people whose books I was reading in secret, who were gay canon to me, you know? So that feels really extraordinary.

LYDIA: They text each other.

I tell them that when we were getting ready to interview them, Billie and I both followed them on social media. We both commented to each other that their life just seems to exude queer joy.

LYDIA: I mean, look, we're definitely a lesbian cliché. Been together forever, have lots of pets. We got so many pairs of Birkenstocks and Blundstones.

CANDY: Lots of Crocs.

LYDIA: I feel like we've like really settled into a very comfortable lesbian middle age. For better or worse.

But, look, I feel like it would be essentially impossible for me to overstate how important to my life our relationship is. It literally is my life. I look at all the things that I've done in my life, and will do in my life, and I honestly struggle to think of anything that I'm prouder of than this marriage and the life that we've built together.

My parents had a really, really bad marriage and should have divorced a lot sooner than they did. And it was really important to me to build a life that was filled with love and joy and togetherness and laughter and care for one another. And so it's a thing that I really want to be known for.

MARILEE LINDEMANN

(SHE/HER)
FOUNDING DIRECTOR
OF THE UNIVERSITY
OF MARYLAND'S LGBTQ
STUDIES PROGRAM

MARTHA NELL SMITH

(SHE/HER)
EMILY DICKINSON
SCHOLAR

ABOUT AN HOUR INTO OUR FIRST INTERVIEW, I'm alone on a Zoom call with Martha. Marilee has ducked out to pick up their takeout—"some sort of Korean fusion"—and I take the lull as an opportunity to ask what she thinks of Mike Hadreas's metaphor: that queer people need more "maps" for our possible futures.

Without taking even a moment to think about it, she points me to two lines by Adrienne Rich.

First, from "Twenty-One Love Poems XII":

> *whatever we do together is pure invention*
>
> *the maps they gave us were out of date*
>
> *by years . . .*

And then from "Transcendental Etude":

> *No one ever told us we had to study our lives,*
>
> *make of our lives a study, as if learning natural history*
>
> *or music*

In the middle of the conversation, Marilee walks back in the door. "Are we quoting Adrienne Rich?" she says, sliding back in front of the screen.

Always ask literary scholars about metaphors.

Martha is arguably the world's leading Emily Dickinson scholar. If you've ever heard that Dickinson was queer, you can thank Martha for that. Her work studying Dickinson's personal letters has shaped the academic understanding of the poet's sexuality since the '90s. And twenty years later, the film *Wild Nights with Emily* starring Molly Shannon and the anachronistic series *Dickinson* have corrected the canon in popular culture. (*Wild Nights* directly credited Martha's work.)

Marilee wrote *the* queer book on Willa Cather—a sapphic author at a moment in American history when "romantic friendships" between women were being recast as "sexual deviance." But these days, she describes herself as an "institution builder." In 2002, she founded the University of Maryland's first LGBTQ studies program and served as its founding director for twelve years.

It should be no surprise that academia brought these two women together. "Love and work have always been intertwined," Marilee says.

MARTHA: We met in graduate school.

MARILEE: We were both in the English PhD program at Rutgers in the early nineties.

MARTHA: She is much, much younger than I am.

MARILEE: She's much, much, much older than I am. When we met, I was twenty-four, about to turn twenty-five. And Martha was thirty, about to turn thirty-one. And so at that point, a six-year age gap, it really did feel like she was much, much older than I was. She was more advanced in the program.

There is almost an academic generational difference between us. I started graduate school in the fall of 1981. And that was an important year in the history of Rutgers English and women's studies at Rutgers because they went out of their way to recruit people to come do feminist work at Rutgers. So it was that moment when Elaine Showalter was in the English department, and Catherine Stimpson would go on to direct my dissertation.

So I was recruited to come do feminist work. And they were offering the very first feminist seminars and courses. Whereas Martha's cohort, just a few years earlier, they were all sort of self-taught as feminists. They had reading and study groups, but the idea of actual seminars in feminist literary theory?

I mean, half the class did start sleeping with one another.

MARTHA: I was not part of this.

In fact, when they met, Martha wasn't available.

MARTHA: Well, I was living with somebody—it was kind of an accident. We had been dating, and we were out on a date, and one of my friends called me at the bar we always went and hung out at and said, "I hope this date is a really good one because our apartment house is burning down."

So I ended up moving in with that woman. I mean, I didn't really have any place to go. She was okay. And we were getting along. [*turns to Marilee*] Okay, well, she wasn't you.

I moved in with her and we lived together for a couple of years. But when I saw this one, I was like, "Huh. Somehow I'm going to hook up with her. I don't know how."

MARILEE: And I was a young, innocent thing—still recovering from the tragedy of my first relationship. And so I was looking at them as like, you know, I had no idea that lesbianism could actually work at this point. But I was committed. Little did I know that I would soon be stealing her away.

MARTHA: That's right.

MARILEE: Our first substantive conversation was in the office of the English graduate program secretary, and we started talking about Martha's dissertation proposal. And forty-five minutes into the conversation, the secretary very gently suggested that we get the hell out of her office. So we went into the mail room, and we continued our conversation, because she was working on this very hot project on Emily Dickinson.

We were both really interested in gender and sexuality. We both have a really strong connection in our intellectual and political commitments. And because she was with somebody else at the time, we were friends before we were lovers. We've been together now for almost thirty-nine years. So either we're just too lazy to get out or—

MARTHA: No. I think it's gonna stick.

MARILEE: I think so. Yeah. I'm feeling good about our chances.

They've lived in the same house since 1994, just a few minutes away from the university. When we arrived, their two wire-haired fox terriers—Max and Maddie—followed us from room to room, offering toys and napping on the backs of couches. The siblings are not Marilee and Martha's first wire-haired fox terriers. First came Roxie. And Roxie "was famous in very specific circles," Marilee says with a twinkle.

Martha pulls out her laptop and looks up "Roxie's World." At Roxies-World.blogspot.com, the terrier wrote about "Politics. Pop culture. Basketball." Marilee built a whole world through the eyes of her smart, empathetic terrier, revolving around Roxie's World Enterprises LLC, complete with a local pub (Ishmael's) and guest appearances from Mark Twain. Marilee was the blog's typist, called Moose— nicknamed after Mussolini because she insisted on teaching Roxie to sit. Martha was called Goose, the fun one. And through that world, Roxie commented on the presidential elections, the state of higher education, and the weather. "It was one of my favorite writing projects," Marilee says.

But the day we are at their house, they pull up a singular episode of *Roxie's World*: the post from the day she passed away. The "Really Most Sincerely Dead Edition" opens at Ishmael's, "the seedy yet cozy bar around the corner from global headquarters of RW Enterprises LLC," where Moose drowned her sorrows in pools of queso. From their couch, Marilee reads it out loud, and all four of us are cackling. "This is why we've been together all this time," Martha says, pointing to the screen.

But by the end, when Mark Twain handed Moose a copy of Robinson Jeffers's poem "The Housedog's Grave," we are all in tears. (And this is before Martha starts mixing Manhattans.)

In another corner of the house, Martha's office could not look more like it belonged to a literary scholar, stacked floor-to-ceiling with books. Emily Dickinson paraphernalia litters the office (she insists she's never purchased a single piece; they're all gifts). I ask Martha what originally drew her to the poet.

MARTHA: From the time I was a little girl, I really loved her poetry. It just takes the top of my head off—as she said about poetry she loved.

I'm also a very detail-oriented scholar, and I happened to notice that she was very persnickety about using the words *published* and *print*. She never said she didn't publish ever, ever, ever. She simply said she didn't print. And so I asked myself the question—maybe she published herself in her letters, coterie-style, like people would do in the eighteenth century, nineteenth century. How many poems did she send

TOP IMAGE: Martha, photographed by Marilee.

BOTTOM IMAGE: Marilee, photographed by Martha.

out in her letters? Lo and behold, about half of her poems—and we've lost a lot of her letters. I decided my dissertation would be studying that correspondence.

We're getting to the queer part.

So, to whom did she send the most letters and poems? Oh! To a woman, Susan Dickinson [her sister-in-law]—of whom everybody told me, "Don't bother with her. She's not important." But if you put books of Emily Dickinson's letters up on a shelf, the ones to Susan would be this thick [*holding her hands a foot apart*], and then the next most thick book would be about maybe a tenth of that size. And so she lavished all of these words: "I could not drink it, Sue, till you had tasted first, though cooler than the water was the thoughtfulness of thirst."

I mean, come on.

Then I noticed that when she's writing about Susan, there were eraser marks and cutouts of some words. And I'm like, "Wait a minute." And so that's how I figured out that someone had come along and tried to erase it.

MARILEE: Martha has, over the last almost-forty years, utterly transformed scholarship on Emily Dickinson—and to some extent, to an important extent, popular perceptions of Emily Dickinson.

Martha is not alone. There have been other people who have been doing similar work. But you've done it in the most disciplined, persistent, and sometimes the loudest and most effective way. I'm just in awe of what she has done. It's had an impact that literary scholarship rarely has, and it has been just glorious to be along for that ride.

Marilee knows what it means to shift literary canon. Her book on Willa Cather, *Queering America*, captures queerness in the subtext of America's "First Lady of Letters," who was otherwise regarded as homophobic and misogynistic (a response, Marilee says, to the rising movement to classify sapphic love as deviant). Martha still assigns the first chapter of her book in her classes. ("She's the very best writer I know, period," Martha says.) But her passion for the last several decades has pivoted.

MARILEE: In my bones, I'm an institution builder. Martha has spent most of her career working on scholarship, and my passion in recent years has really been institution-building. At a place like Maryland, you're holding the institution accountable for its own rhetoric about diversity and inclusion.

She built the university's first LGBTQ studies program, effectively from scratch. Taking inspiration from the early feminist studies programs she came up in, she turned a mirror on the university and challenged them to explain *why* they wouldn't have a queer studies program.

MARILEE: You have to ask, "How can you not have an LGBT studies program? All the other cool places have one." That's sort of how we played it, and it worked. It was my privilege to direct it for twelve years.

MARTHA: You're a visionary. You're a very practical visionary. And those are the visionaries we need because those are the visionaries who actually make change.

More than once in our conversation, they stop to tell me how important being visible was to them.

MARILEE: It's always been important to us—

MARTHA: Visibility is crucial.

MARILEE: —to be as out as we can be, because we have that privilege. And with that privilege comes great responsibility.

Since stepping down from the LGBTQ studies program, Marilee has been the director of the university's College Park Scholars program.

MARILEE: We have a convocation ceremony at the beginning of the year. And in the last couple of years, I have worked in a line of my speech at that ceremony, where I come out to all nine hundred students at once. And it's because I know there are gay kids out there, and I know that they come from places that aren't as safe and comfortable as the University of Maryland. And it's very important for me to let them know that I'm here, I'm queer, and I'm there for them.

Both of them know what it's like to come from environments that aren't as friendly as the University of Maryland.

MARILEE: When we were coming up, it was much harder for a parent to be confident that their child actually could be happy living a gay life.

Martha's family were fundamentalist Christians. "It was a cult," she says. "To the right of the Baptist church." She originally married a man from the same church.

MARTHA: Right before I got married to the other person, the male person, my father stayed up very late to talk to me, which was uncharacteristic of him. And he said, "I'm gonna say one thing to you. And I'm only going to say it once, okay?" He said, "He is a lovely man, but he's not smart enough for you."

When she came out, they cut her off and disowned her for a while. Then they met Marilee.

MARTHA: At some point, my dad got me isolated and said, "She can hold her own with you. She's smart enough for you." Both of my parents knew that when we got together, this is the love of my life. They knew, and they knew I was very happy. They could see. They adored her.

MARILEE: That's because I'm adorable!

I ask Marilee if she came from a similar environment.

IT'S ALWAYS BEEN
IMPORTANT TO US
TO BE AS OUT AS WE
CAN BE, BECAUSE
WE HAVE THAT
PRIVILEGE. AND WITH
THAT PRIVILEGE
COMES GREAT
RESPONSIBILITY.

—*Marilee Lindemann*

MARILEE: It was a differently conservative environment. The conservatism was not really religious. I grew up in Indiana, so it was a kind of classic middle-class, small-town conservatism.

My parents did raise me to be very independent. They were people who believe that if you have a God-given talent, you have an obligation to develop it as much as you can. I was smart, so success in school was expected of me.

My mother was a high school English teacher, and she had four kids. My parents were one of the original dual-career couples. So, in other ways, there were some very progressive things about it.

Both Marilee and Martha had closeted gay friends when they were growing up, but Marilee's first real exposure to queerness was at the end of high school.

MARILEE: The summer between my junior and senior year of high school, I participated in a language immersion program that Indiana University sponsored. So I spent the summer in France speaking French and realizing that there is no God in the universe, right?

And so I just became impossibly bohemian and cool. And I had teacher crushes—that was my queer childhood. One of the teachers in this immersion program was named Giselle, and I have a memory of the two of us walking arm in arm in Paris, because she bonded pretty tightly with me too—it wasn't just a one-way crush. So we're walking arm in arm, and here I am, this little hayseed kid from Indiana—and she laughed and she said in French: "People will think we're dykes." She used a slang term—*gouine*—which I didn't understand. So I had to ask her.

She explained to me, and I fiercely responded to her: "I don't give a damn!" That was my first experience of any kind of queer consciousness, where I said I don't care what people think. And that's really the story of my queer life.

She brought that attitude home when she started getting ready to tell her parents about her sexuality.

MARILEE: I think they were really, really nervous in my last year in college when I came home reading *The Dialectic of Sex* at the breakfast table, and I had grown out all of my body hair—man, I had some hairy legs on me when I was young—and I think that they were sort of freaking out that—where is this all leading?

As far as I was concerned, they had always said, "To thine own self be true." So, as far as I was concerned, when I was ready to announce my sexuality, they should have said, "Well, good for you, kiddo." And they freaked out.

My mother threatened to kill herself the night she found out I was a lesbian. It was fairly dramatic. She went through the motions of having a nervous breakdown that summer, but I knew that it would pass because that's the way my mother was.

But I think I always knew that, in the end, they would come around. As long as I'm professionally successful and personally happy, I knew that they would be fine with whatever. And they met Martha, and they liked her because she, too, is adorable.

Once their lives were fully immersed in academia, though, they never negotiated queerness and visibility again. As long as they've been together, their relationship has been loud and proud.

Together, they've been on the entire legal journey of gay marriage. In 1989, they threw a huge commitment ceremony with 150 of their friends. The invitation called the party "Practically a Wedding." And on March 8, 2014, after the Edie Windsor case was decided in the Supreme Court, they got married in the same living room where they read *Roxie's World* to us. ("Largely because the caterer was available on three weeks' notice," Marilee says.) You can still see the marks on the floor where they dragged their piano in for the ceremony. Marilee sang "Grow Old with Me" by John Lennon as part of her vows. There wasn't a dry eye in the house. "It had the desired effect," Marilee says.

But they don't use the term *wife*. "It's not reclaimable for me, personally," Marilee says. *Spouse* is okay; *partner* is better. They're two people who revel in the written word, so perhaps it's the ways they write about each other that matter most. For my part, I'm partial to a turn of phrase from another one of Marilee's blogs: Much like *Roxie's World*, it's now defunct, but for years, she wrote a post with the same title for their anniversary. Their fortieth is coming up, and this year, it would have been titled "Forty Years of Queer Delight."

BEN BARNZ

(HE/HIM)
PRODUCER

DANIEL BARNZ

(HE/HIM)
DIRECTOR
AND WRITER

"ARE WE GOING BACK IN TIME?" Ben asks Daniel.

I just asked how they met. There's a long version and a short version, they say. Which did I want?

In the short version, Daniel was doing his graduate work at the University of Southern California's film school. He was making a short and he cast Ben in it.

BEN: It sounds tawdry, but it really wasn't.

DANIEL: It was not tawdry.

"That's actually how we met," Daniel says. But the long version is better.

Years after Daniel cast Ben in his short, they were at a play at the Public Theater in New York City. "We were sitting there. And then Ben said, 'Oh, I know that casting director,'" Daniel tells me. "And I said, 'Oh, I have a funny story about that casting director!' And then I proceed to tell him the story."

In college, he had spent a summer living in New York with his brother. He had started to take a serious interest in acting, so he'd gotten headshots and "somehow got connected with an agent."

DANIEL: In the fall, the agent called me up and they said, "Oh, they're doing a new Neil Simon play on Broadway. And you're gonna come and audition for it." So I went to New York. But the thing was, I was maybe nineteen at the time, and the role was for a thirteen- or fourteen-year-old. So I had to dress down—slick down my hair and wear big tie and a vest and whatever. I realized I was running late for the audition, so I ran down the subway, jumped over the turnstile—because I couldn't wait on line—stepped on the train and felt a *tap, tap, tap* on my back. And it was the MTA. And they arrested me for jumping a turnstile. And then I spent the next six hours handcuffed to a seat on a New York City public bus because the jails were too full.

I was sitting next to this guy named Socrates. And then two rows behind me was a guy named Wisdom. And Socrates and Wisdom start having this conversation about me, because I was dressed to look like a fourteen-year-old, and they were like, "What's he doing on the bus? What did you get arrested for?"

Anyway, I missed the audition. I went back to college, and then about a couple weeks later, the agent called me up and he said, "Look, they're at callbacks, and they really have a good feeling about you, so you're gonna go straight to callbacks." I went in; I did it. And there were three people who were up for the role. One of them was me. One of them was the person who got the role. And then the third, as it turns out, was Ben.

BEN: He has a better story than I do. I took a subway. And I paid for it.

Self-portrait by Ben and Daniel.

The Barnzes have such a defined rhythm in their storytelling. Ben is a producer and Daniel is a writer and director. Together, they run We're Not Brothers Productions, and the industry permeates their household. When we meet them at their home in Los Angeles, they have been in the writers' room for a new project and are buzzing with the excitement of a new story.

Perhaps the only thing that thrills them more is their family. On the wall in their living room, they have a framed, handstitched family crest with all of their faces: Ben; Daniel; their daughter, Zelda; and their son, Dashiell. It reads: "The First Family of Fabulous: In Humor We Trust."

Some key context for their family motto: "We're a fully queer household," Daniel says, grinning. Both of their kids are adopted, so for them, it feels like the universe did some big gay magic. "For them to come from different families and then end up in our house—as queer people—it feels like there is a great queer god looking out for us."

But it also took a lot of work.

Daniel, photographed by Ben.

Ben, photographed by Daniel.

In the '90s, getting married wasn't yet an option, but Ben and Daniel did everything but. They started with a commitment ceremony in Vermont in 1999, then opted for domestic partnership in California as soon as it was recognized. "Then we did a kind of ceremonial thing with our family and friends," Daniel says, "and then shortly after that we decided that we wanted to adopt children." A hyphenated name sounded tedious, so they took letters from each of their names, came up with "Barnz," and found an adoption attorney.

BEN: You have to fill out pages and pages of questions. Who are you? Where do you come from? What kind of child-rearing did you have? What kind do you want to have with your family?

It was infuriating at the time, he says, because he was acutely aware that most straight couples didn't have to go through that to start building a family. "Excuse my French, but—fucking straight couples have sex, and she's like, 'I'm pregnant.' And then they're like, 'Let's just do it.'" But it had a silver lining: "We really had to sit down and really talk about what we wanted our family to look like before we even had a family."

The hoops didn't end there, though.

DANIEL: You also have to put together a book [for birth parents who might choose you to adopt their baby]—photographs of your life. Our adoption lawyer had a really specific format. The cover picture had to be the two of us with our arms around each other, touching each other. And then the caption had to read "Your baby will have two loving dads."
It has to be very up-front. "This is a queer family," but also, it's a loving family.

BEN: Part of the subtext was "You will always be the only mother."

DANIEL: And it was interesting, because even at that time—in the late nineties—that itself felt a little radical and scary. It was kind of exciting that you're sending this book out to some random person and that you have no idea kind of what their belief systems are, but you have to show yourselves holding each other.

They'd been warned that it could be a long time before a birth parent chose them, so they got started in their twenties.

DANIEL: I liked the idea of being a young dad. And particularly for two men, it could be really hard. We had lesbian friends who would pretend to be single mothers, but it was a little more complicated as two men. So we began the process because we thought, well, this will probably be like three or four years down the road. And then six months later Zelda's birth mom was in Los Angeles.

And with that, their life started to take root.

Their production company came a few years later. Zelda was four, Dashiell was two, and Daniel had been writing fairly successfully in Hollywood for about a decade. But nothing that he was working on was taking off.

BEN: He said, "I need to have a movie—where I'm directing—within a year, or I would like for us to pick ourselves up and move to Africa for a year and just sort of shake it all up and see what happens."

DANIEL: I just got really obsessed with elephant orphanages. And I had a vision that we would go and live in Africa and work in an elephant orphanage.

BEN: Which, one part of me was like, "That's totally fucking cool. And I'm sort of down for it." And then part of me was like, "We have a two- and a four-year-old and that sounds really daunting."

He had this script called *Phoebe in Wonderland* that I had always loved that he wrote in grad school. And I was like, I'm gonna produce this movie because I'm not ready to move to Africa with my two- and four-year-old. And I had never produced before, so I took the script, and then I figured out a cast for it and got a cast. And we were in production within ten months from him saying that. That's how we became partners.

Their relationship stumped folks in Hollywood at first.

DANIEL: Our names were appearing on call sheets together—both as Barnz—there really wasn't much of a precedent for same-sex couples having the same last name. So people assumed that we were brothers because there is a big precedent for brother filmmaking duos— Coen brothers and a whole bunch of others. So people would just assume that we were brothers, then they would see us on set like not really interacting quite the way that brothers would. And then we named our production company We're Not Brothers Productions to make it really clear.

Even so, not everybody gets the joke. "Some people actually think it's ironic," Daniel says, "and they assume that we actually are brothers. And we were in one meeting where we had definitely talked about our kids earlier in the meeting. And then later in the meeting, they said, 'Wait a second, you're not brothers?'"

It's a theme, for Ben, at least—feeling like you're perpetually coming out.

BEN: Maybe I'm totally wrong, but it feels like our kids came out and it was sort of done. They told everybody, and everybody knew. When we were coming out, you would come out in dribs and drabs. You told your one friend. And then you would tell someone else and then you'd sort of go back a little. [*he turns to Daniel*] Do you have a coming-out story, Dan?

DANIEL: Well, I was *very* out in college but not to my family. But I am one of four children, and three of us are gay.

My sister came out first, then me, and then my brother. It was interesting because our parents are incredibly politically progressive, but contending with their children's sexuality was trickier—particularly, I think, for their male children, because it was 1993. It was so close on the heels of the AIDS epidemic, so to them, coming out meant death.

I was living in San Francisco, and I wrote a letter to my parents declaring my bisexuality. And they wrote back, "Maybe you lean more toward the straight part." And then I had to write back another letter being like, "I totally lied to you in the first letter. I'm actually kind of gay."

Acceptance was a slow process. "My father was an editor, and years later I found the letter that I had written him," Daniel says. It was covered with notes. Some correcting his grammar and some asking, "what does this mean?" "And it had arguments against [my queerness] too."

Their son, Dashiell, came out in an entirely different world, but there are still some delightful parallels between his and his dad's coming-out stories. Ben and Daniel actually debate who would get to tell me the story. Daniel wins.

DANIEL: Before our kids would fall asleep, we'd lie down with them and have a little chat or talk about the day. And this was when Dashiell was thirteen, right before he decided that that was never going to happen again.

I was lying down with him, and he was in this weird mood. He was sort of chatty but not chatty at the same time. And I had this crushing work deadline the next day. And then I went upstairs, and ten minutes later, he called for me to come down.

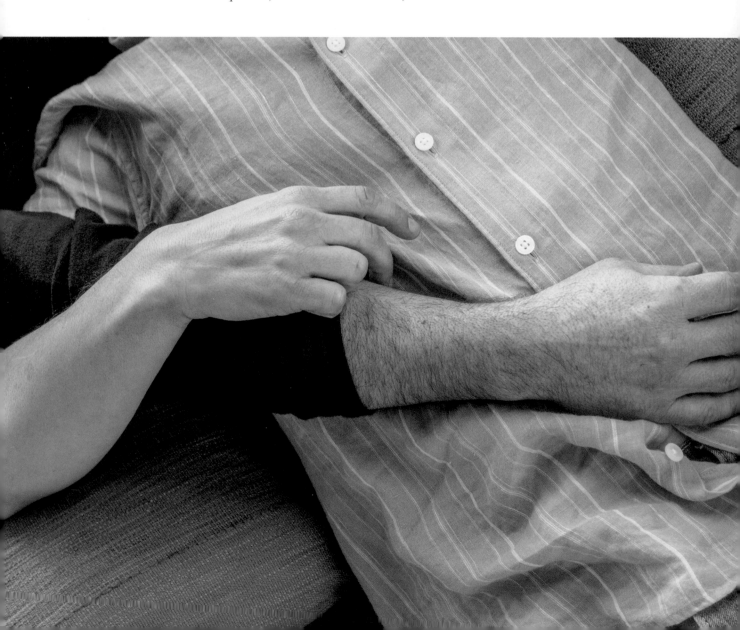

And it's hard to explain what this feeling is when you've gone through so many years of putting your kids to sleep and then they call you down to their room afterward, when you finally feel like, "Okay, I'm gonna have an hour to myself."

I went down. And he was like, "Um, can we go to Starbucks in the morning?"

By the second time Dashiell called him downstairs, Daniel's stress was bubbling to the surface. He told Dashiell that if he wanted to talk, he had to come upstairs to talk to him.

DANIEL: So he comes upstairs, he pulls out a little Post-it pad from our kitchen drawer, and he writes something down, and then he left it on the counter. He went back down to his room, and I walked over to check it, and it said, "I'm gay. Text me any questions you have." And that was how our son kind of came out to us.

I ran down and showed Ben the note, and then we went up and gave him a big hug. But that felt like an incredibly Gen Z way to come out, on a Post-it note.

The couple has kept Dashiell's Post-it and Daniel's letter with his dad's edits as treasured coming-out artifacts—marking the importance of the occasions. But their kids were less precious. When everyone woke up in the morning, Dashiell texted the family group texts for both sides of the family and told everyone he was gay and then headed to his carpool.

BEN: Daniel and I were home and our kids were in school together. And we texted Zelda and said, "Can you do us a favor? Can you just check on Dashiell and see how he's doing?" And she wrote back, "Why?" And we realized in that moment, the difference between our coming out and their coming out—she didn't even understand why we were asking if he needed to be checked on. He was totally fine—it couldn't be less traumatic.

Zelda came out soon after Dashiell, completing the First Family of Fabulous.

DANIEL: Shortly after that, Zelda started coming home with these stories about the Rainbow Alliance at her school. The characters would be, like, the class president who was openly queer and would show up wearing heels but was also like the head of ten different committees.

She kept telling these stories, and we encouraged her to write them down. And then somehow at some point, one of us said, "You know, it actually would make an interesting world for a television show." And that was the germ for what became *Generation*.

Though I have to stress that Zelda was only fifteen—we didn't in any universe conceive that it actually would be a show that would get made. We just thought that was a really fun way for us to connect with our daughter.

In talking about the show with Zelda, she realized that for the show to work, she'd have to be really honest about what it was like for her to be queer, what her friend group looked like. And so, in the context of talking about the show, she became really open about talking about her experience.

And so we started having these really frank conversations with her, and then Dashiell became part of the conversations too. So suddenly, the four of us were these four queer people sitting around our kitchen counter—where we usually eat dinner—having these, like, wildly candid conversations about sex, sexuality, and identity that I never in a million years would have had with my parents. And it was so refreshing and inspiring. Occasionally really embarrassing, but pretty spectacular.

Several cast members came out while they were working on *Generation*, and the Barnzes started to extend the First Family. "They actually kind of became part of our family," Ben says. "Like a real extended family."

I ask them if being queer, and having queer kids, feels like having a secret language in their family—a shorthand that most families aren't lucky enough to have.

DANIEL: Being queer opens up pathways of communication, for sure, but it doesn't prevent generational gaps. It doesn't stop your kids from just feeling like you're their old dad.

BEN: You're still their dad.

But that dynamic still profoundly shapes their kids' lives and their own.

DANIEL: When we look at the various miracles and blessings that have unfolded in our life—the fact that our daughter had this idea for a show that was about a lot of queer kids, and especially queer kids of color, and that then prompted us to kind of go down a journey, which then resulted in a show being on the air that was about queerness—that was just a real gift. And it's really interesting to think about how that has shaped our direction now—that we feel very, very passionate and invested in—not only in terms of creating content that celebrates and has queer representation but also that particularly leans into queer joy.

They're able to do that offscreen as well.

BEN: We went to visit our daughter in college, and she lives with a bunch of queer people. And she was like, "This one guy, I really want him to see you." But I think so many kids have not seen two men together who have raised kids. And it's interesting to me when our kids sort of want to show us off in that way.

DANIEL: You too can be old, boring gay dads.

PROFESSIONAL QUEERS

WHEN WE DECIDED TO MAKE THIS BOOK, there was one particular question we knew we wanted to ask: What does it mean to the people in these pages to be a "queer power couple"? How do they relate to being role models in the LGBTQ community?

The question led us to possibly the most famous married gay man in the United States—Jim Obergefell, the plaintiff in *Obergefell v. Hodges*, the Supreme Court case that made same-sex marriage the law of the land.

"I never once thought about being a Professional Gay," he tells me, laughing. "Or a well-known gay? It just wasn't something I ever considered, and then it happened!"

159

He met his husband, John Arthur, at a house party in Cleveland. John was his coming-out affair, "but we never once hid it," he says. In 2011, they'd been together for nearly two decades. They had a house together—and some elder gay neighbors that they considered their own role models—but they weren't married. Then John got sick. In 2013, as John's health declined, they got married in Maryland—where same-sex marriage was recognized—on the tarmac in a medevac plane. But because Ohio had a same-sex marriage ban on the books, Jim wouldn't be listed on John's death certificate as his spouse, leaving him without any of the protections or benefits that a spouse receives when their partner dies.

So they sued. And though John would pass away before the case was decided, in 2015 their marriage became the most famous gay marriage in the country.

I ask Jim if he realized that this case would turn him into a public figure. "I do remember thinking, 'Am I ready to say in the news that I'm a gay man?' and very quickly going, 'Why not?'" he tells me.

Since the case was decided, he's consistently reminded of the importance of that decision: He remembers parents in Philadelphia asking if they could take a photo of him with their kid, "because thanks to you, we know that he'll be able to marry whomever it is they love"; and a young woman at the University of Tennessee who told him that if it weren't for the *Obergefell* decision, she might not have made it to adulthood. "It's weird to have my last name be shorthand for marriage equality," Jim says. "But I'll take it. I'll take my name being mispronounced. I'll put up with hearing it come out of the mouths of people who hate us, because I was part of making the world a better place."

When we asked the couples in this book how they relate to being queer role models, each one of them seemed to take it seriously. They weren't uniformly enthusiastic, ("I'd prefer not to be visible," Roxane Gay was quick to say, "but I think that everyone has responsibilities in a functional society, and if this is one of those responsibilities, then so be it") but they all recognize the power that they have and the newness of that power.

Queer role models not only demonstrate that out, thriving queer people deserve to take up space—they make space for more of us. Andria Wilson Mirza works with Sundance to improve LGBTQ representation in film and crews. Chani Nicholas and Sonya Passi have built an astrology empire that centers queerness and progressive issues. Sean and Terry Torrington create Black, queer content—while setting an example of what queer marriages can look like after separation. Charlie Jane Anders and Annalee Newitz reimagine queerness thousands of years in the future.

There is an abundance of queer excellence. And the more that excellence exists in the public eye, the more maps or torches or possible selves we have. "If you're out there being you," Jim says, "unapologetically you—you're a role model to someone."

QUEER ROLE
MODELS NOT ONLY
DEMONSTRATE THAT
OUT, THRIVING QUEER
PEOPLE DESERVE TO
TAKE UP SPACE—THEY
MAKE SPACE FOR
MORE OF US.

SEAN TORRINGTON

(HE/HIM)
CO-FOUNDER
OF SLAY TV

TERRY TORRINGTON

(HE/HIM)
CO-FOUNDER
OF SLAY TV

WHEN WE FIRST STARTED working on this book, every few weeks I would google "queer power couples"—I wanted to see who people were talking about, who'd gotten together, who'd broken up. While I scrolled, Sean and Terry Torrington almost always popped up. The co-founders of Slay TV, a streaming network dedicated to Black queer entertainment, had been celebrated by *Out* magazine and NBC and seemed to always exist in the public eye together. So in early 2021, we reached out, excited to talk to them about their experience with running the platform as a couple.

"Terry and I have been separated for some time now," Sean wrote back. But he wasn't declining our request for an interview. "We've maintained our relationship while running our business and still have so much love for each other . . . and are now as close as family," he wrote. "Is there still space to be a part of this book?"

They ended up being our first interview. Sean said that their "journey of uncoupling is just as valuable as being a couple." And we figured, if this project was about finding maps of queer futures, separating is one of those maps.

It's easy to conflate the Torringtons with their network, because in a way, Slay TV starts where their relationship starts.

They don't agree on all the details of how they met—"Who spotted who first?" Terry says. "There's always gonna be two different versions"—but they do agree on a couple of things: They met on the dance floor at a house party in Brooklyn and a guy named Mush was involved.

TERRY: My version is that I spotted him first, because I was in the kitchen with my friend Mush. We were getting drinks, and I saw Sean come into the kitchen, greeting people, making his rounds, being the mayor. He smiled, and I'm like, "Oh, he has a really cute smile." And that was it. And later on in that evening, I was on the dance floor, you know, with my Corona, just doing my little two-step, and my friend Mush tapped me and I turned around and Sean is there. He's like, "Sean, this is Terry. Terry, this is Sean."

It wasn't his first Corona that night, so the memory is a little blurry, but he does remember Sean's phone: It was 2010, and Sean had one of the first touch-screen smartphones. "He had the brightness all the way up, so the phone nearly blinds me," he says. "He does this still to this day."

SEAN: Okay, so before Terry even comes to the party, I already had it down—I was gonna find my boyfriend that night. Because I was tired of being single.

TERRY: I'm not gonna lie. When I went to that party that night, I was on the opposite end of the spectrum from Sean. I'm going out to have fun. Because I had just started talking to a guy that wasted my time. And I'm like, "Fuck all this dating stuff. I'm young. I'm single. Let me just have fun." And then I met him. And then here we are eleven years later.

SEAN: There's the weed room, and then there's the area where people were dancing, and then there's the kitchen where there's drinks. So, as I took my last pull, I said, "All right, I'm gonna be on the prowl." So as I'm shuffling through the crowd, I see Terry. I spotted him because he had very, very nice teeth. And I'm a teeth person. So I was like, "Okay, he's dark-skinned. He has nice teeth. And he looks like me."

I saw Mush. I just asked him, "Is that your boyfriend?" So Mush just turns around: "Terry, this is Sean. Sean, this is Terry." I was just like, "Oh, my God, that is so corny."

They agree to disagree on who saw who first. And ultimately, it didn't matter. In their web series *Love @ First Night*—which is based on that night at that party—they caught each other's eyes at the same time: Terry in the kitchen, Sean on the dance floor. It became Slay TV's first show.

When they announced their new streaming service—"the premiere destination for Black, queer, and trans entertainment"—the word *husband* was in the headline of almost every article about them. They were photographed together, interviewed together—their relationship was a character in their story.

SEAN: In the beginning, it was the coolest thing to have Black queer people be represented in media. And you didn't see that representation a lot in 2010. Slowly but surely, though, the community was putting us on this pedestal of, like, "relationship goals."

TERRY: Like a fish in a fish tank. At first it was cool. But then after a while, it felt like a performance.
     Before I met Sean, I was very much not out to my family and to close friends and stuff. But I always make the joke that Sean is the mayor of the Black queer community in New York City. So everyone knows who he is. And then we started working together creatively—working through video, and press, and things like that, and it just started to become a normal part of my life.

SEAN: For me personally, we were really showing representation of two first-generation, masc-presenting, West Indian, dark-skinned Black men. You don't ever see this.

TERRY: And it showed a lot, because sometimes we'll be out on the train and an old lady would be staring at us. And she'd be like, "Are you two brothers?" Sean will be the one that'd be like, "No, this is my man." And people just get this weird, like, shock. It was always the same reaction every single time.

Sean never formally came out, he says. "I came out to myself at thirteen, and I would say I came out to my family—which, they should have always knew—but I would officially say nineteen." And he dove into queer culture as soon as he had access to it. "I've been in the community since I was fourteen. My first time on Christopher Street, I was fourteen years old." But Terry was fresher.

TERRY: I came out three times: the first time at twenty-one, with my parents—I was actually outed, because my aunt found some things on the computer and decided to tell my father; and then came out to my friends around twenty-three; and then twenty-five was when I officially came out to the whole family. So it was a very short period of time before I met Sean. And I wanted a boyfriend, but I didn't realize, I guess, what that entailed. Sean is very big on PDA, and I didn't realize how uncomfortable I was with it. This is still something I'm actually working through—him being so free and open, saying, "This is my boyfriend." You remember, Sean? I used to mumble, "Oh, this is my friend Sean."

It was a challenge, because Sean has a very big personality. And when he wants to do something, he goes for it. And I wasn't necessarily used to that. But I liked it.

I think the biggest thing for me is that Sean gave me permission to unapologetically be an artist. And so I trusted whatever he wanted to do. But at the same time, I didn't realize how bad my anxiety was. And so a lot of times, it was like, "This is too much too soon."

In person, you can see the remains of that dynamic. Terry's still a little quieter, hanging back, while Sean practically two-steps down the sidewalk. Terry called him the mayor of the Black queer community, but it seems like he's the mayor anywhere he goes. Walking through Brooklyn's Flatbush neighborhood, he stops to talk to someone he knows on almost every block. Terry doesn't look anxious or uncomfortable anymore, though, just entertained.

We met them at a classic Brooklyn row house on a street lined with linden trees. It's Sean's family home—housing several generations of his relatives. He and Terry lived here together for years, tucked into a small bedroom in the early days of Slay TV.

Sean still lives here—in a different room from the one they had shared—and Terry visits often. Today, it's to cut Sean's hair. Terry's still the only one he'll trust to clean up his edges.

It's been three years since they separated, and they're clearly still figuring out the contours of their relationship. Because of Slay TV, their separation was never going to be a clean break, and it gave them an opportunity to pick and choose the parts of their marriage they wanted to hold close and the parts they'd grown out of.

SEAN: Nothing has ever really changed in my eyes. We just don't sleep with each other. We speak to each other every day. Because we have such a bond and such a great friendship—and we are family, first and foremost—on my end, I don't feel like anything has really been missed. He's always been my best friend.

TERRY: Within the separation, there's been a lot of self-discovery on my end—me trying to step into more roles or doing things differently, and us trying to meet in the middle. Because even before we separated, we're both artists, both creative. So ultimately, we're going to clash. Just trying to get through that moment and really get to the meat and potatoes of what's happening is the challenge. But for the most part, I think we both have the same vision as it relates to Slay TV, and that's where we find that common ground and just create from that space.

It's like we share custody of this child that we created together.

They're still the Torringtons—Sean took Terry's name when they got married, and he has no interest in giving it back. They're still regulars at the same restaurant they always went to—a vegan spot on Nostrand Avenue called Aunts et Uncles—and everyone there still recognizes them as a unit.

"And secondly," Sean says, "we're still married."

TERRY: I try to explain this to everyone—we're still together but in a different capacity. It's still like family—I still check in on him and listen to stories about what's going on with his family and vice versa.

SEAN: Most people that we have spoken to are like, "How do you do that? I can never be friends with my ex." I'm like, "Were you friends from the beginning?" It's that unconditional love, knowing that, no matter what, this person has my back.

Staying married also means they can stay kin in a literal, legal sense.

SEAN: I know that I can trust this person with my life, so that's why I'm not pushing to go get divorced. Because who else is gonna be responsible for me? This is my person. He knows exactly what would happen if I was to get hit by a bus. He's the only person who knows these things.

TERRY: Not to get it twisted; we still get on each other's nerves. And there'll be moments with a silent treatment, but we always come back, just like a relative. If it's your brother or sister getting on your nerves, you're like, "I can't talk to you right now." But we're always able to come together, talk it out, and move forward.

SEAN: When we were in a relationship, it was seven minutes later and might be seven hours later, but you know, we still come back.

Throughout our conversations, we talk a lot about the intersection of their queerness with the hyper-masculinity and homophobia that they encountered in West Indian culture.

In particular, it meant that they had no access to any semblance of queer imagery. So they found it wherever they could.

TERRY: It was Lamar Latrell from *Revenge of the Nerds*. Lamar was the first person I recognized as queer. I wanted to be him. I was probably like four or five when I saw that. And that embodiment of him—it made me know it was okay to just be so colorful, because he was so different. And it was normal—watching my family watch it and just laugh at him, it's just like, it's on TV, so it's okay. He was my gay icon growing up, before I even knew what gay was.

Terry, photographed by Sean.

Sean, photographed by Terry.

SEAN: I don't know if I had a queer icon growing up—I think I'd spend so much time running away from that part of myself that I didn't. It was the divas at the time that really felt like icons to me—Mariah Carey and Whitney Houston—just seeing them free in their femininity and being fabulous in sparkly dresses and singing, that really woke it up for me.

The first person I recognized as queer—I was in kindergarten. And there was this boy that was more feminine than I was. And I knew right away that was a connection—that was somebody that I just wanted to be friends with.

And I'm going to tell you a story, and this is dead-ass the truth. He went to the bathroom, and I said I wanted a bathroom pass to go to the bathroom too. And I don't know for the life of me how we ended up in the stalls, and we was kissing in the stalls. In kindergarten.

TERRY: That is very on-brand for you.

SEAN: And we got caught. The teacher came in and caught us and told our parents that we were kissing. I would never forget that.

Acceptance was a slow roll for both of their families.

TERRY: My father said he already knew. All he said to me was, "Don't beat yourself up about it. It's not your fault. Just don't embarrass me." Whatever that meant. To this day, I still I don't know what he meant by that.

SEAN: My mother said the same thing.

TERRY: It's probably a Caribbean thing. With my mother, the part with her was more the "devastation," because she's like, "Oh, you're not going to give me grandchildren."

But for the next generation, they've had a chance to crack open some doors in their families.

SEAN: My nephew is queer. I kind of knew at a very young age. I knew when he was four because, when we was in the room voguing and stuff, like, he was so fascinated with it. And me, his mother, and my friends would be voguing, and he would try to vogue. And now he's voguing at balls.

TERRY: He's twenty-three. He is so amazing.

When I first came out, my mother was like, "You know, it kind of makes sense, because your father did tell me that he slept with a man before. But I didn't believe him because I just thought that he was being silly."

I never asked him about it because they were separated for years. And when I came out, I thought he didn't know until, ten years later, we was on the phone, and he was like, "I know you think I don't know. But I know. But I just want to let you know I don't care because I think you're dope. My son is really fresh. You dress your ass off. So just keep doing what you're doing." And I was just like, "Okay."

Spending time with them, it was clear that Sean and Terry have a lot of the same shorthand. They credit it to being two Black, masc, dark-skinned, first-generation, West Indian gay men in the same industry; they move through similar worlds in similar ways.

Another factor, I think, is that they've both clearly grown so much because of each other.

SEAN: I learned the power of being still and doing the inner work and seeing that someone can actually heal from certain traumas. This journey that Terry went through—I've seen him become this kind of illustrious being. And I'm like, "Wow, he's in a different plane right now. I need purpose."

TERRY: When I first met Sean, I was rough around the edges. I did not care about attention to detail. Sean taught me the importance of quality and paying attention to the small details. I took a lot of Sean's eye.

One of the places they chose for their photo shoot was Brooklyn's Prospect Park. They go there to brainstorm—talk out story ideas and rough patches in their scripts.

They bring a picnic blanket and bag full of crystals to let them charge in the midsummer sun. Sean leads the way as they walk us to their spot—a hidden outcropping by the lake with a small wooden shelter surrounded by towering trees.

I am struck by how deliberately they build their space still. It reflects the generous space they make for each other in their lives. I ask them how, specifically, they hold space for each other in their worlds as they pull apart.

SEAN: I hold space for just listening and just being a listening ear when he needs to vent. And just being there. Present, not just listening, but being present and being responsive.

TERRY: I think the space I hold for Sean is for healing. I feel like throughout the duration of our relationship, and even after the separation, I've just been able to observe certain things in his life. And because I'm very big on healing, I'm very big on self-care and things like that. And I know Sean's potential. I already feel like he's a powerful person, but if you were to spend some time, really look into the things that happen in your life, and whatever triggers you may have, you will be even more unstoppable. And I feel like there is a bit of fear of him looking at those things. And I realized that I can be a bit pushy with it. So I tried not to do too much. But I definitely do hold space for his healing.

As the morning sun turns to afternoon, they pack up their crystals and take shelter under the wooden structure. They sit next to each other, mirroring their body language and talking through a problem with their most recent series—a rhythm that seems as natural to them now as it always has been.

TERRY: There's no pretending when it comes to each other. It's like one of those relationships where I do feel safe to make mistakes and to have a bad day or whatever, because we know each other. I don't have to overexplain anything about myself. Certain things are known and don't have to be said. We just support each other in a way that isn't conditional.

SEAN: Terry just said it all. I just feel like our relationship is kind of full. We just created our own relationship.

CHARLIE JANE ANDERS

(SHE/HER)
AUTHOR

ANNALEE NEWITZ

(THEY/THEM)
AUTHOR

ONE OF THE EARLIEST RULES in Annalee and Charlie Jane's relationship was: There are no sidekicks.

Even on first google, it's pretty apparent that there are no sidekicks between them. Charlie Jane is a speculative sci-fi writer and the author of the Unstoppable trilogy. Her other books include *All the Birds in the Sky* and *Never Say You Can't Survive*. Annalee is also a sci-fi author, as well as a science journalist. They have been equally celebrated for their nonfiction explorations of mass extinctions as for their science fiction novels. Together, the two founded and ran the publication *io9* for seven years. And between them, their bookshelves hold two Lambda Awards, five Hugo Awards, an *L.A. Times* Book Prize, and a Nebula Award, just to name a few.

But their "no sidekicks" rule goes back more than twenty years. "We're switch-kicks!" Charlie Jane says. "It's one of our patented terms."

ANNALEE: We had couples counseling early in our relationship. And our biggest issue was the fact that we're both in the same field—we're both writers, we work together a lot—and we're often dealing with the same forms of anxiety: A book is about to come out, or I'm trying to sell a book, or I'm trying to make people pay attention to this article.

CHARLIE JANE: It can be so easy to just let them feed on each other.

ANNALEE: We spiral, and we end up reinforcing each other's anxiety.

It's a thread through a lot of the conversations in this book: learning how to make space for each other when *your thing* is the most important thing in the room, but so is theirs. But no one else shared quite such a perfect term for their solution. One person can't always support the other—can't always be the sidekick—so they switch. "Switch-kicks!"

ANNALEE: The piece of advice that we learned in therapy that we still use now is: We can't both talk about our anxieties at the same time. Otherwise, it gets really dark. But we have this super-basic structure: Charlie will say to me, "I really need to talk about my thing right now." And I'll be like, "I'm gonna put my thing in a box, and we're only gonna talk about your thing." And then we can switch. It is super simple. And I guarantee it's the reason we're still partners.

CHARLIE JANE: It's just the ability to take turns.
I actually find it kind of soothing for myself to be that voice that's like, "I'm gonna give you a reality check. You're doing really well. And yeah, this thing sucks. But on the other hand, look at all these other wonderful things!" It can be really

therapeutic for me, because it's hard to do that for yourself sometimes, but it's easier to do that for another person.

ANNALEE: It's a way of being like, "Wait, there's a part of me that's not the scared, anxious person. There's the other part of me that's ready to take on anything."

Obviously, it's not perfect. We're like any other couple, and we're still perfecting that advice that we got long ago: No sidekicks, just switch-kicks.

Their dynamic is especially fitting, I think, because they've been each other's fans since day one. They met in the late '90s at San Francisco Sex Information, a local nonprofit.

CHARLIE JANE: We were taking the sex educator training together, and we just started hanging out. And I remember Annalee was telling me about their PhD thesis about Marxism and horror movies and capitalism [author's note: It's called *Pretend We're Dead*, with choice chapter titles like "Mad Doctors: Professional Middle-Class Jobs Make You Lose Your Mind"] and I was just like, "Wow, oh, my God," and I just started following them around. I was just totally smitten.

ANNALEE: This was in 1999. I had just graduated, which is why I was trying to impress girls with my PhD thesis. And Charlie Jane told me that she had created this website called God Hates Figs, which at the time was a huge meme. It was making fun of the Westboro Baptist Church, whose slogan was God Hates F*gs. This whole website was about how figs were evil, and it was full of quotes from the Bible. And so when she told me that I was like, "What the hell? You created one of my favorite joke sites?"

So we were in this very intense class, and it goes on for several weeks. And I would try to sit by Charlie, but I felt like she didn't want to sit with me. I just thought that she was a little bit too cool for me, which is totally true. And I kept being like, "Oh, she doesn't really like me. She just doesn't think I'm very cool."

CHARLIE JANE: Oh, my God, nothing could have been further from the truth. I was in a complicated situation at the time. I was just starting my transition. I was experimenting with different kinds of femme presentation: Did I want to be gender-fluid? Was I genderqueer? It was a complicated time for me gender-wise. And I had just come out of kind of a difficult breakup. But honestly, my feeling at the time was that I had been trying to hang out with Annalee at every possible moment during this training. We would sit together at lunch or whatever. And I felt like they were ignoring me.

ANNALEE: [*laughing*] I would sit with you and you would, like, move away.

CHARLIE JANE: Because I felt like I was coming on too strong! And I still have all the agonized emails I sent to my best friend, like, "Oh, my God, how do I know if they like me?"

ANNALEE: We were friends for at least a year.

CHARLIE JANE: Nine months, I'm gonna say.

ANNALEE: And we were both writers. And I was an editor and I commissioned some stories from Charlie, because I thought she was talented. I just thought, "Oh, we're casual friends, and I really admire her work."

And then at some point, we went out for dinner. And again, I was just like, "Oh, we're having like a collegial dinner with this writer who I work with." And Charlie's like, "Well, I guess I should just tell you—" I can't remember your exact words.

CHARLIE JANE: I said I was in love with you.

I was emailing my best friend, and I was like, "I'm going to tell Annalee I'm in love with them." And my friend was like, "Don't do it. That's a terrible idea." "But if I don't do it, I'm gonna regret it for the rest of my life. And I just, I love them so much. And I just can't stop thinking about them." And they were like, "Okay, go for it. No guts, no glory."

I still have all those emails somewhere.

ANNALEE: I mean, I wasn't mad about it. I was just so shocked because this whole time I was like, "Yeah, she totally doesn't like me that much." And we were in line at this place where they had little chairs outside, and I was so shocked that I literally had to sit down. I've never had that happen in my life.

And so, that said, that was how we started dating.

CHARLIE JANE: I think it actually took a few months.

ANNALEE: Because I was so surprised! Because of course, I did think Charlie was super hot and wonderful and stuff. But I had worked so hard to categorize her as Just a Friend.

But it was nice, actually. I really liked the fact that we started the relationship with the pure emotional honesty of like, "I really care about you," and not kind of with like, "Oh, are we going to *like* like each other or not?" The whole goal is that we really, really love each other. And we're just going to try to figure out how to be partners, instead of just, like, weirdo nerds who don't know how to express their feelings.

CHARLIE JANE: I just felt like this was the person I wanted to spend my life with. And this was my person.

The awkward few months ended on Charlie Jane's birthday in 2000.

CHARLIE JANE: A friend of ours just decided to be a bit of a yenta, and just was like, "Let's get dim sum for Charlie Jane's birthday." And then the friend was just like, "Okay, I'm gonna take off now," and just kind of bailed on us.

We ended up just hanging out for the rest of the day. And I always say that this was the best birthday of my life. That was the birthday when my life changed forever. That was in the summer of 2000.

ANNALEE: And we've been pretty much inseparable since then.

And because they started working together during those awkward few months, they've been professionally inseparable for just as long. "We did some wacky performances together" early on, Annalee says. (Namely, an event called "The Ballerina Pie Fight.") In 2008, they co-founded *io9*, the Gawker-owned blog about science fiction, fantasy, futurism, science, and technology; and in 2018 they started the Hugo Award–winning *Our Opinions Are Correct*, a podcast that explores "the meaning of science fiction and how it's relevant to real-life science and society." But their collaborative relationship, they say, really began in 2002 with *Other: The Magazine for People Who Defy Categories.*

ANNALEE: We did a lot of great work on it. And I think that was how we learned to collaborate. Charlie Jane is much better at outreach and getting people excited. I'm much more excited talking about "What is going to be the editorial direction of this publication?" and "How are we going to ideologically align ourselves?" And Charlie's like, "How are we gonna get people to dance?" And I love that. Like, I want to dance. So I feel like when you put us together, we're two people who want to dance! But have good politics at the same time.

CHARLIE JANE: Awesome things happen when we work together. We did *Other* magazine, we did *She's Such a Geek* [an anthology of women writing about science and technology], we did a bunch of other little projects together. And then we did this website, *io9*.

But from the summer of 2015 until sometime in 2018, Annalee and I did not have a project we were doing together. And I remember saying that this is the first time that we've been in a relationship but not collaborating on anything! So it was actually nice, because there were times when that firewall I've tried to keep up so work didn't bleed into our relationship—that was a challenge. And so I was like, "Okay, maybe it's a good thing to have a few years of us not collaborating on anything so that we can have a reset and really get to know each other again as partners, without being coworkers." And so I'm really glad we did that.

And eventually, after a few years, we started talking about how we miss collaborating. And it wasn't like it was an economic necessity, or like our careers were languishing. It was purely just that we missed collaborating, and we missed having a project we were doing together, because we really enjoy that.

We saw that our relationship was wonderful without collaborating on a project. And we were both really happy with where our relationship was. But it's just an extra dimension. And it was just fun. And so that was when we decided to do [*Our Opinions Are Correct*].

ANNALEE: But our podcast is the diametric opposite of *io9*. We don't make any money from it. It's just for the love.

When we meet them in person, it becomes instantly clear that that is true. Within seconds of sitting at a table together, they dive into a conversation about an obscure sci-fi author, with banter that could have easily been recorded for their podcast. (They say they use a script for the show, but they clearly don't need it.) As decades-long collaborators, I figure they are also each other's best cheerleader, so I ask what they love about each other's work.

CHARLIE JANE: The thing I love about Annalee's nonfiction is that they draw connections between things that you might not think are connected. They're really good at uncovering interesting, strange, unexpected discoveries.

And their writing often deals with really upsetting, horrifying stuff—but they always have this undercurrent of tenderness. In their fiction, they often write about characters who are in high-stress violent situations and dealing with intense moral quandaries. And there's a thread running through their fiction of chattel slavery and corporate abuse, and people being denied their full personhood. But at the same time, their newest book, *The Terraformers*, has some of the most beautiful,

TOP IMAGE: Charlie Jane, photographed by Annalee.

BOTTOM IMAGE: Annalee, photographed by Charlie Jane.

unexpected love stories that I've seen in a long time. And I just I love the way they write about people and about systems—

ANNALEE: Okay, I'm gonna talk about you now! When I first met Charlie, one of the main ways that I knew about her work was through her performances. She would always give deranged comedy interludes between each section, which were surreal and whimsical, and just bonkers. Charlie can get on a stage and just make the room love her, and it's so wonderful to watch. (And also to know that I actually get to go home with her.) And so I think the first thing that I loved about Charlie's work was that kind of pyrotechnic whimsy.

And when she started writing novels, it really came through, but it became much, much deeper. The first novel of hers that was published was called *Choir Boy*. And it's about a trans teenager, very much ahead of its time. What year did that come out?

CHARLIE JANE: 2005.

ANNALEE: I really love that book! It's about a trans teenager who's struggling with a lot of shit. It's really dark and kind of violent but also incredibly silly. And Charlie's always been able to balance a lightness and a whimsy with incredibly profound philosophical insights. She has these insights into human psychology. I don't even think you know how smart you are, Charlie Jane.

She's been telling me what she's writing about for this next book. And at one point, Charlie was saying, "You know, when people feel deeply guilty about something, they always think they're guilty about the wrong thing. They never realize what they've actually done wrong." And I was like, "Holy fuck, that is so true."

And then as you're reading the story, it's slowly dawning on you that this is where she's taking you as a reader. Half the book, you're just dazzled by magic. And then by the end, you're like, "Oh, this is actually about this really smart insight about what it means to be guilt ridden, and why guilt never results in relief."

The other throughline in both of their work, perhaps unsurprisingly, is queerness. When I first met Charlie Jane and Annalee, Marvel had just released *Marvel Voices: Pride (Vol. 2) #1.* The comic debuted Shela Sexton a.k.a. Escapade, a trans mutant superhero and a member of the New Mutants—a spinoff of the original X-Men. In interviews, Charlie Jane described Escapade as "a total goofball with a super-strong sense of justice and a profound loyalty to her friends." And she emphasized that being a mutant was not a metaphor for being trans. Instead, Escapade; her best friend, Morgan Red (who's also trans); and a genetically engineered flying turtle named Hibbert lean into the queer experience of chosen family.

Still, Charlie Jane has a somewhat fraught relationship with leading with her identity—when we first spoke, she told me she was working on an essay for her newsletter about how she "burned out" on presenting herself as a queer and trans writer. Lately, instead, she talks about the idea of "ambient queerness" in her work: the idea that queerness doesn't have to be explicit—or worse, tokenized—in a story to be understood.

CHARLIE JANE: I feel like I'm so steeped in queer culture, and I'm so steeped in my community, that it's gonna bleed through no matter what. And it's true that sometimes I find it really powerful to write things that are metaphorically trans or metaphorically queer. In my novel *The City in the Middle of the Night,* the characters are actually explicitly queer on the page, but they're not trans on the page. And there's one character who goes through a major surgery that people read as being a metaphor for trans surgeries. And I think that there is something to that—I think that I like to do both, I like to do things that are the "speaking to the choir" experience, and also things that are just like, "Here's a queer character and here's their life."

I feel like what I've been able to do recently that I've been really having fun with is actually doing both in the same work—having characters who are metaphorically trans or metaphorically queer, next to characters who are actually trans or actually queer.

For Annalee, that "ambient queerness" has been infused into their work as long as they can remember.

ANNALEE: I've been openly queer ever since I realized I was bi in high school, which was, in retrospect, not a great idea. I grew up in a very conservative place, in Irvine in Orange County, California. It was Reagan country, very evangelical Christian. When I first came out, I had one friend who was gay. And we wanted to go to the local queer community center, which was constantly being firebombed. And so the week we got up our nerve to go, it had gotten firebombed that week. And so we're like, "I guess we'll just go next week!" And that was just that place at that time.

I had a really hard time not just being queer, because it was, I think, probably pretty obvious to everybody. I guess [my work] has always been kind of ambiently queer, even when I was not writing explicitly about queer things.

But I will say that as I've gotten older, and as the culture has changed around me—thank goodness for people starting to have nonbinary identities, because I've always been nonbinary. There just wasn't a word for it in 1985.

So as things have changed, I feel like I've gotten more legible. I feel like people can actually see who I am now. And it's not just like, "Who's that weird girl-boy thing?" No, it's a nonbinary person.

My first novel was about a gender-confused robot who goes from using he/him pronouns to she/her pronouns. And it was really my effort, I realized later, to talk about being nonbinary. And I came out as nonbinary shortly after that.

And then in my most recent novel, *The Terraformers*, like 75 percent of the characters are nonbinary. And it almost doesn't matter. Because they're robots, they're moose, they're cats, they're trains. These are not *Homo sapiens* characters, so it makes sense that their pronouns wouldn't be *Homo sapiens*–type pronouns.

Charlie Jane talks about science fiction as dreaming: "You don't predict the future," she said in her TED Talk in 2020. "You imagine the future." Annalee's sci-fi imagines a future where our current conversation about sex and gender are beside the point.

ANNALEE: How do we expand our notion of personhood so far beyond today that these petty notions of male and female just become absurd? Like when you're having a conversation with a train, whether or not the train is male or female is like, "Who gives a fuck? Why are you having a conversation with a train?" In the book, you will find out why you're having a conversation with the train—because the train is a person.

I really like to just always try to be taking it to the next step. Now we have nonbinary identity. Now we can all be trans. All right, so when do we all get to be friends with moose? When do we get to have a conversation with the trees?

But while Annalee's fiction is planted firmly in possible futures, their nonfiction trails across time and space, from the past (*Four Lost Cities: A Secret of the Urban Age*), to the future (*Scatter, Adapt, and Remember: How Humans Will Survive a Mass Extinction*), to our present non-moose-related experiences of gender and sexuality ("Love Unlimited: The Polyamorists").

All their work is clearly rooted in curiosity and deep-diving research. And for their photo shoot, they asked us to meet them at the Prelinger Library in San Francisco—a research collection of "nineteenth- and twentieth-century historical ephemera, periodicals, maps, and books." (Their favorite gray archival box of the day was titled "Math/Oddball Science/Science Fiction." It shared a shelf with "Radical Psychiatry" and "Space History" Boxes 1–3.) The library is on the third floor of a sprawling warehouse, tucked next to a pole-dancing studio. (If you go at the right time, you can hear the bass through the walls.) Twenty years ago, Annalee and Charlie Jane came to this library to pull inspiration for *Other* magazine from old zines and periodicals, and Annalee often comes back when they're diving into a new project.

They arrive a few minutes apart, hustling from their respective apartments. The two have always kept their own places, and they've always been poly, Annalee says. Their apartments are a thirty-minute walk apart. It's a really lovely walk, they say, and they're big walkers. They only mentioned their "pod" in passing, but their polycule often gets a nod in their books' acknowledgments. (Annalee calls them their "lifelong sweeties.")

At the library, Annalee seems just as at home in the stacks on "Oddball Science" as "Public Land Use." It might be a product of their upbring: Despite growing up in Reagan territory, Annalee's parents were liberal democrats—both teachers who loved literature and were dedicated to their largely immigrant students—and they made a point to expose Annalee to as much culture and literature as they could when they were growing up. That also meant really deliberately exposing them to queerness as a kid. The first person Annalee recognized as queer was Harvey Milk, because their parents took them to see a documentary about him after his death.

Charlie Jane, however, grew up in rural Connecticut, in a small college town, where she didn't even know to look for queerness yet.

CHARLIE JANE: I was bullied a lot in school. I was non-neurotypical, and I had a really, really, really severe learning disability. I was a very weird kid. And I think that I wasn't conscious of being queer for most of that time. But I think people could tell that I seemed to be queer?

It was not always super fun, and it took me a long time to come out—first as bisexual, in my early twenties, and I became poly at some point in my early twenties, and then came out as trans a little bit later. It was a really long and difficult process, because I had really struggled with my identity when I was younger and was really unsure of where I fit in. I think the fact that I was kind of stigmatized for other stuff—for my learning disability and for just being kind of a weirdo in general—made it harder for me to come out.

I sort of clung to certain ideas of being "normal" for a long time, because I felt so not-normal in a lot of ways.

ANNALEE: I sometimes fantasize that we could have been in the same high school, and I could have totally protected you from those shitheads. We would have teamed up. And we would have hung out with a gang of nerds.

I formally request that that be the premise of their next novel.

At the end of our conversation, I (once again) share Mike Hadreas's notion that we historically haven't had enough queer maps. At the intersection of their identities—bi, trans, nonbinary, poly—does that feel true to them?

ANNALEE: I think that's such a good metaphor, because especially in our generation, we didn't have any elders who were modeling happy queer life. When I was coming up, I was mostly around gay men, and it would just be like, "Gay men don't have long-term relationships." And I was like, "Well, why?"

And being polyamorous makes it even more complicated. I think that often overlaps with queer identity—I think there's a lot of poly queer people. And you're just making your own map. You're like, "Okay, what feels good? I literally don't know."

That's why I like to write a lot of characters who are robots or non-human animals who are learning to have sex, because I feel like that was my experience. I'm in this body. People keep telling me what I'm supposed to do with it. And literally none of the instructions work. And so I just have to start from the first principles. "Does this feel good? Does that feel good?" And that's why I like robots! Because robots can be very methodical about it. "All right, we will go through this subroutine. Does that feel enjoyable? What about this one?" And so I was just lucky that I found a lot of nerdy people to have sex with because they were like, "I, too, am completely confused. We will confuse each other together."

Twenty-three years later, they seem to have their footing. But even if they're a little bit less awkward than they were when they were avoiding each other at the San Francisco Sex Information trainings, they're no less obsessed with each other—their relationship is a little beacon of queer joy.

CHARLIE JANE: I was just the most smitten I've ever been in my life. And I'm still totally smitten with Annalee.

ANNALEE: I knew that she was the greatest ever, but like, spending the past twenty-three years of my life with her, she's just gotten cooler. In fact, you're cooler than you were yesterday.

ROXANE GAY

(SHE/HER)
AUTHOR

DEBBIE MILLMAN

(SHE/HER)
DESIGNER

IT TOOK EIGHTEEN MONTHS, four emails, a recommendation from a friend, and some really good luck for Debbie Millman to get Roxane Gay to go on a date with her.

In 2017, Debbie's résumé was a list of superlatives: one of only five women to ever be named president emeritus of the American Institute of Graphic Arts, the co-founder and chair of the School of Visual Arts' branding program, and the host of the first and longest-running design podcast, *Design Matters*. But Roxane had no idea who she was.

Roxane had her own laundry list of titles: professor, celebrated cultural critic, *New York Times* bestselling author. She'd recently published *Hunger: A Memoir of (My) Body*—a story of sexual assault, body image, and, as she put it, "what it's like to live in a world that tries to discipline unruly bodies." The *Times* called it "luminous." The *New York Review of Books* called it "unerring." To Debbie, it was how she first fell in love with Roxane.

After reading it, she wrote to Roxane—a long, soul-bearing message telling her how much the book had moved her. Roxane never responded; and it seems like Debbie took that as a challenge. For more than a year, Debbie sent her thoughtful, eloquent letters about her work, describing what her books meant to her. And every time, she was lucky if she got a full sentence from Roxane in response. Until finally, after a year and a half, she asked Roxane on a date, and Roxane said, "Sure."

When I talk to them four years later, they are in their home in New York, and they've been married for ten months. The pandemic turned what was once meant to be "the fantasy," as Roxane put it—with four hundred guests, officiated by Gloria Steinem—into a quickie wedding under a plastic chuppah officiated by a Russian woman from InstantMarriageLA.com.

Debbie recently came across that first email she sent Roxane on June 17, 2017. She wasn't coming onto her, she insisted. But she wasn't *not* coming onto her either.

ROXANE: It was a lovely letter.

DEBBIE: It was lovely—I bared my soul to her!

ROXANE: And I did not bare my soul back. I barely acknowledged it.

DEBBIE: *Barely* acknowledged. I wrote this whole long thing, quoting the book, expressing how I felt about what she's written about certain things, about scar tissue. And she wrote back, "Oh, I'm glad my book impacted you the way it did" or something like that. That was it! And then I wrote again. And at the time, it was like two days after I had broken up with my ex. It wasn't a pickup letter; it was just an appreciation letter.

ROXANE: It was a pickup letter.

DEBBIE: In any case, three months later, she had written something in the *Times* about *To Kill a Mockingbird*, and she got a lot of vitriol on Twitter about it. And I wrote her about that. And she again wrote me back a sort of one-line thing. And then she had done a podcast in Australia and was treated really meanly, so I wrote her again about that. And then the fourth time I wrote, a year later, a mutual friend of ours, [author] Ashley Ford, sort of helped grease the wheels of my being legitimate to Roxane. But it really wasn't until a good six months after that. I was very gently but persistently—

ROXANE: *Very* persistently.

DEBBIE: —showing up.

ROXANE: She really went all out. I have to say, nobody has ever pursued me as consistently and ardently as Debbie did.

And I was just like, this lady's weird, and it's super intense. I was actually in a relationship at the time—a complicated relationship where I could see other people, but nonetheless, I wasn't really looking. So I didn't even realize that she was into me. You have to really spell it out with me—I am not going to read the tea leaves and fucking read between the lines. Unless you're not interested in me, and then I will read between the lines and imagine things that aren't there.

DEBBIE: She made me work really hard. It was June of 2018 when I wrote her and asked her on a proper date. I had to make it really clear: "I'm asking you out." And she wrote back, "Sure, next time I'm in New York, let's do something. Let's have a drink." That was it. A *one-liner*.

ROXANE: And I never gave a time or a date.

DEBBIE: So at this point, I didn't want to overwhelm Roxane, so I didn't know how to ask when she was going to be in New York. But I followed her on Twitter, and a fan asked, "Roxane, when are you going to come to Podunk?" and she said her schedule was on her website. And I saw that she was going to be in New York in October. So I wrote her back, "Would you like to have a drink? I'll come to the event, and we can go for a drink after."

WHEN PEOPLE GET TO KNOW YOU THROUGH YOUR WRITING, THEY TEND TO THINK THAT'S THE WHOLE OF YOU. AND SO I WOULD CONSTANTLY WORRY, "IS SHE GONNA FIND OUT SOMETHING ABOUT ME THAT DOESN'T JIVE WITH WHO SHE THINKS I AM BASED ON *HUNGER*?"

—Roxane Gay

ROXANE: And at the time, I was just like, "Whatever." And it ended up working out!

DEBBIE: [*laughing*] We're fucking married!

ROXANE: Yeah, it was intense. I mean, I just had never been pursued, and especially by someone who I could introduce to my family without cringing.

      So it was overwhelming and surreal. She came to one of my events, and I didn't google her, so I didn't know who she was or what she looked like. So during the signing line, I would just evaluate every woman who walked up in the line to decide, like, is this someone I would like to have sex with?

DEBBIE: She's really like a teenage boy.

ROXANE: But awesome, and I don't smell. And there were a couple of women who I was like, "Not for me"—but I mean, the Lord enjoys us all—and then she was the very last person in line.

DEBBIE: Intentionally. I'd let everybody go ahead of me.

ROXANE: And then I was like, "Oh, she's mega hot." And she was slammin' hot that night. And so we ended up having a lovely, lovely time. And the more I got to know her, I thought, "This is a really lovely person. She's incredibly intelligent. She's funny—"

DEBBIE: Go on.

ROXANE: "—and she's fascinating."

DEBBIE: Go on.

ROXANE: "She's beautiful."

DEBBIE: Go on, go on.

ROXANE: And it was great. I was a little nervous, because when people get to know you through your writing, they tend to think that's the whole of you. And so I would constantly worry, "Is she gonna find out something about me that doesn't jive with who she thinks I am based on *Hunger*?" But she was willing to get to know me beyond the page. And it was important for me that she understands that that's me in the book, but it's not *all* of me.

Roxane and Debbie were both already well known, and already out, but their relationship really pushed their queerness into the public eye. "It was really a 'one plus one equals three' kind of thing," Debbie says. "People seemed to really celebrate our union." As someone who once relished the anonymity of the online chat rooms of the early aughts, Roxane oscillates between embracing her visibility and resenting it. But Debbie had come out just a few years before they met and could still easily summon up that fear and the challenge of imagining what queer life and love and happiness look like.

DEBBIE: I'm fifteen years older than Roxane. I didn't come out until I was fifty, and I'm about to turn sixty, so it's only been ten years. Seeing how gay people were treated in society is part of the reason it took me so long to come out. I was already so insecure and so self-loathing that the idea of being any more different than anybody else than I already felt was just more than I could bear.

Debbie grew up in Brooklyn in the '60s and '70s: The Stonewall Riots were one borough over when she was nine years old; the first Pride march happened the year after that. Gay sex was illegal in New York until she was nineteen—and only became legal nationwide when she was forty-two. She started to question her sexuality almost perfectly in the middle of that timeline.

DEBBIE: I suspected, sort of semiconsciously, that I might be gay in my senior year of college. I was a reporter, and I was doing a piece on the LGB—well, I wouldn't say it was called the LGBTQ community at the time but just gay and lesbian people—and I interviewed a prominent activist lesbian on campus. And I remember thinking, "This is what feels like home to me." I wasn't attracted to her, and I wasn't interested in her. But the whole way that she was living her life felt very intrinsic to me. It was the first time I'd ever felt that way, and it was a very deep, powerful feeling—so much so that forty years later, I still remember it.

   I moved to Manhattan after I graduated, and I felt very attracted to the West Village scene, to the women bars—Cubbyhole and Henrietta's, places like that. I would frequent them by myself anonymously. None of my friends knew. There was a gay and lesbian bookstore right across the street from where I lived, and I was buying Ann Bannon novels and reading under the covers with a flashlight. But I really didn't do anything more with those feelings—or suspicions—until after two failed marriages to men and a lot of therapy.

   And because I had spent most of my adult life feeling like there was this part of me that I wasn't expressing, whenever I was around gay women, I would always sort of *nod-nod, wink-wink*. Not that I was coming onto them; I just wanted them to recognize something in me.

ROXANE: Did you wear a big *L* on your chest?

DEBBIE: No.

ROXANE: You should have!

DEBBIE: I wanted to! Because I wanted them to know that I was one of them, even though I wasn't able to express that. There was this dog trainer who trained my dogs in the early aughts, and she was gay, and all of the women that worked for her were gay. And I loved being around them. And again, my *wink-wink, nod-nod* went unnoticed.

   But I was always much more—I don't know what the word is—just comfortable and happier and in my own self around gay women. So when I came out, there was all this time to make up. Being out and proud became a way to acknowledge all of that hiding.

Even though she's only been out for a decade, Debbie still comes off as a queer elder. She's built a robust queer community—many of whom she was eager to recommend for this book—and even during an interview, she exudes a sort of protective, maternal energy that seems rooted in sheer queer confidence.

   That confidence could be, in part, thanks to Roxane, who has been grounded in her queerness for as long as she can remember.

TOP IMAGE: Debbie, photographed by Roxane.

BOTTOM IMAGE: Roxane, photographed by Debbie , with their dog, Max.

ROXANE: For me, I actually never had any angst about my sexuality, which I'm so grateful for, because I had angst about literally everything else. I just accepted it. I was like, "Yeah, women are hot. I'm into this." And when I came out, it was complicated, because in many ways I was trying to push my family away. And so I kind of used coming out as a weapon. And it didn't work, because my family was like, "This isn't our favorite thing, but whatever. We love you." How dare they.

   And so I'm very fortunate that it was never mired in any sort of self-loathing. But I do know that there still were very few examples. I didn't know any other queer people in my family yet. And so I didn't have any role models. The role models I did have I found in the community in Lincoln, Nebraska. And the community was grounded around this great little bar called the Panic Bar. And so a lot of what I learned about how to be queer was from older women in that community. There was this one couple, Pat and Joy, and they were both normal, middle-class, Midwestern lesbians. And it was really interesting to see—they'd been together, at that point, for eighteen years. It blew my mind. I didn't even know that was possible. And so it was great to see that. I just wish I'd had more of it because they were literally the only lesbian couple I had ever seen.

   But I definitely never thought that visibility mattered until we did this event at Autostraddle's A-Camp. And these young women kept coming up to us after our event, thanking us for being visible. And when I saw what it meant to all of these young women, I realized that we don't actually have a lot of examples of prominent lesbian couples who live in the public eye.

   I'd prefer not to be visible. But I think that everyone has responsibilities in a functional society. And if this is one of those responsibilities, then so be it. And I think it's great for people to see healthy, happy relationships between women. A lot of times, queer narratives, especially from the time that I grew up, are that our lives are kind of miserable. And they're not, actually.

Despite seeming to know nothing about Debbie's career before they met, Roxane is now just as awestruck by Debbie as Debbie was by her four years ago. ("She's like, 'Oh, I just have to do an event with the biggest furniture designer in the world,' no big deal," Roxane teases. "That's her life every single day. It's hilarious and incredibly hot.") They're both quick to say that the other works too much, but they also seem to like that about each other. Roxane puts it simply: "She makes me want to do the work." Thanks to Covid restrictions, by the time we got on our call together, they'd spent the last four hundred days together (Roxane: "But who's counting?") mostly isolated in their LA home. Despite the chaos, their work isn't at odds with their home life—it's a part of it. "We parallel work a lot," Debbie says. "We're cohabitating and coworking. It's definitely part of the world we've built together."

DEBBIE: If one of us wasn't as committed to our work as the other, I think there would definitely be an imbalance. I think we're equally committed to our work—we're highly compatible in that way. Really compatible in general, in terms of what we like to do, what we don't like to do, when we sleep, when we don't sleep.

ROXANE: We're both night owls, so that helps. And we both have very high-powered, demanding careers. And I think we both acknowledge that we're married to workaholics, and our workaholism manifests in different ways: Debbie works constantly, and I work late. [*laughs*]

DEBBIE: [*crinkling her nose*] You work constantly too, babe.

ROXANE: Okay. [*whispers*] Not as much as her.

DEBBIE: She just doesn't count reading as work.

ROXANE: She will do Zoom meetings and phone calls from nine a.m. to six thirty, pause for dinner, and then she'll do even more until one a.m. Her work ethic is unparalleled. It has blown my mind. I'm just like, "What is wrong with you? Stop!"

DEBBIE: Well, the other part of this is, I didn't achieve any kind of recognition for my work until I was in my forties. It's been a long time coming for me to have opportunities that I only ever fantasized about. So I'm not really working, you know? I'm doing things that I love. And that takes effort and work, but it's not laborious. It's not something I'm dreading or cursing. I'm having fun; I'm enjoying myself. I'm making art and doing podcasts. I'm doing things that are in the top five things that I love doing. So in the same way that you wouldn't consider reading "work," I wouldn't consider some of the things that I do work either.

Plus, I'm still in the mindset that if I don't say yes to everything, I'll never have anything ever again.

ROXANE: Same. So that's part of the reason we're both so overworked.

It's no surprise that they both agree that their type is "brilliance." "My type is someone who's able to blow my mind on a regular basis with their intelligence," says Debbie. "With Roxane, it's empirical. The whole world knows." When Roxane talks about Debbie, though, she gets this Grinch smile that looks like she's a kid who's gotten away with something. "I don't really have a type," Roxane says. "I have many types. I'm the United Nations of love." Debbie chimes in with "She's an equal-opportunity lover" before they dissolve into giggles.

ROXANE: But is Debbie my type? Absolutely.

DEBBIE: Really?

ROXANE: Yeah!

DEBBIE: Okay, I thought you were making fun.

ROXANE: No! You're definitely my type! You're fucking hot!

It takes a while for the giggles to die down.

ROXANE: Debbie has taught me what it means to love someone twenty-four hours a day, seven days a week. Like, the constancy of love—to give it and to be open to receiving it. She's just always there; she's never wavered in her love. Whether she's angry or cranky or happy or melancholy, she still treats me as the center of her gravity. And that's extraordinary. And so that makes me want to rise to the occasion and to be able to reflect that back to her so that she knows that I can always be the still point in her turning world.

DEBBIE: See, how can you not fall in love with that?

Roxane is the only person I've ever been my whole self with. One hundred percent my whole self. I can tell her anything; I can say anything. I can do anything. I can be anything. I can completely tell her the truth, and I don't feel judged.

ROXANE: In our first several dates, she was just like, "This is who I am. These are my issues." She kind of laid out the whole shebang. I think we were both committed from the first date to seeing where this could go and taking it seriously. And it was really satisfying to be with someone who knew what she wanted and then was willing to put in the work. And it was just really lovely that she was able to lay out all these things, because in turn, that made me feel like maybe I could trust this and lay out all of my little specialties and quirks.

DEBBIE: Part of it was influenced by a friend of mine, a gay woman who was married and was experiencing marital difficulties. When she first met and married her wife, for a lot of really understandable reasons, her wife hadn't been fully up-front with her about some of her sexual trauma and how it had affected her. Seeing my friend go through the grief of realizing that this was something that she was going to have to accommodate in their marriage—it was so hard for her to imagine living the rest of her life like that.

So when I was talking to my friend about falling in love with Roxane, in the beginning of our relationship when everyone is on their best behavior, I felt like I owed it to Roxane to be very clear about what some of my issues were and give her the option to want to be with a person like that or not. And that was really hard. But I did it.

ROXANE: She did. It was so ballsy. I give her credit—Debbie is a force to be reckoned with.

DEBBIE: But it was scary! Because at that point, she could have said, "Oh, that's a dealbreaker."

ROXANE: But it wasn't! At first, I was stunned that someone could be that radically honest and just be that open about their issues. This would surprise her, but I didn't for one second consider not dating her. I think the only thing I may have asked was, "Is this something you're willing to work on?" and the answer was yes. And to her credit, we both have things that we're working on. She asked me to go to therapy twice a week, and so I do.

DEBBIE: I just know how much of a difference it makes!

ROXANE: And so I just thought, as long as we're always going to be willing to work on our issues, both individually, and whatever issues arise as a couple, let's go for it.

It's really challenging to be in a relationship with someone who's static when you're dynamic and moving and changing. And so to be with someone who was committed to dynamism and changing and working on themselves was great. And it just gives you so much hope. Because I'm not in this alone. I'm not going to carry the burden of doing the work alone.

Debbie is so hypercompetent that sometimes I'm just like, "Wow, she doesn't need me at all." Which is useful! You're not supposed to need someone. But then I think we also do need each other.

DEBBIE: Absolutely. I need you desperately.

ROXANE: But I know that she can function on her own. As can I. We both came as fully formed adults who can clean a toilet.

It's a benefit of patience. They met later in life, but both of them celebrate crossing paths when they did—when they were ready to be the partner that the other deserved.

DEBBIE: I feel like I'm with my soulmate, and I didn't find Roxane until I was fifty-seven.

ROXANE: And Debbie is definitely my soulmate. And I didn't find her until I was forty-four. And I think it's great. I wish more people understood the beauty of waiting. Even though I had a lot of lonely times, I must say, in my twenties and thirties and early forties. At least now I feel like it was worth it. And it was all leading toward something. I wish more people understood that you can bounce around and have some fun in your twenties and thirties, but you're also probably doing some of the work that could really make you capable of being a great, great partner to someone and to allow someone to be a great partner to you.

You do sacrifice something, and for us it was children. We talked about it early on, and Debbie's worried about her age—I'm not worried about her age in any way—but we've had a lot of conversations about it, and I think the route we're going to go is to foster children.

DEBBIE: Maybe.

ROXANE: Maybe. Because there are so many kids that just need a temporary safe place where "We're not going to bother you, Peter or Mary. You're safe here." I think we have a lot of love to give.

There are things that you get, and things that you don't, but this was well worth it. I have not one single regret.

CHANI NICHOLAS

(SHE/HER)
ASTROLOGER, AUTHOR,
AND, PRESIDENT
OF CHANI INC.

SONYA PASSI

(SHE/HER)
FOUNDER AND CEO OF
FREEFROM, AND
CO-FOUNDER AND
CEO OF CHANI INC.

WHEN I RECORDED THE INTERVIEWS for this book, I loaded all the files into a program that automatically transcribed them. It used AI, so they were always messy—it usually mistook *queer* for *clear*—and every time, after hours of tidying them up, I questioned whether or not it was faster than just transcribing them myself. But one feature it did offer was a summary of the "themes" of the interview—words that came up most often in the conversation. Most of them included *gay* or *lesbian* or *coming out*, maybe something about role models or world-building.

In Chani and Sonya's interview, one of their most common words was *exhilarating*.

It's an unusual word to come up more than once in a conversation, so I searched for it in the transcript. Both of them used it, separately and unprompted, in the same way: to describe what it's like to work with each other.

Chani and Sonya might be the most professionally intertwined couple in this book. On the face of it, they have two very distinct careers: Chani is a writer and astrologer whose work deftly combines horoscopes and star charts with progressive politics and human rights. Sonya is the founder of FreeFrom, a nonprofit that creates pathways to financial security for survivors of gender-based violence.

But Sonya is literally the CEO of Chani Inc., which runs the astrology app that's a new, massive platform for the horoscopes and writings that turned Chani into a queer household name. And Chani Inc., they estimate, has helped raise more than a million dollars for FreeFrom. "We work together every single day on every single piece of every single thing that we do," Sonya says.

In their sun-soaked kitchen in Los Angeles, they sort of buzz around each other, lobbing ideas back and forth across the kitchen island. Chani brainstorms while she sautés leeks and ghee at the stove, and Sonya draws elaborate mind maps at the breakfast counter. It's almost impossible to see where their professional life ends and their relationship begins.

It seems fitting, then, that before they met, their professional lives were almost unrecognizable compared to what they are today.

They met in 2014, when Sonya was an investment banker and Chani was writing horoscopes part-time while teaching yoga. Sonya took a weeklong vacation in Los Angeles, she tells me. "I hadn't taken any time off, including Christmas Day, since I started. And so this was my big one week off." She arrived in LA, "and like any investment banker, I decided that the way I was going to relax was to do yoga every morning at seven a.m." She went to the concierge and asked them to book her a session every morning. The first day, she met Chani.

SONYA: We had one session together, and at the time, it was nothing more than just I really liked her. And I really enjoyed the yoga. So I went to the front desk after my first session, and I was like, "I would like to be with that person for the rest of the week."

Three or four days in, I started to feel things—not understanding what I was feeling. Nothing happened while I was in LA, but on the plane on the way home, I was like, "This is the person I'm going to spend the rest of my life with."

All of this is true. But Chani is quick to fill in some blanks about those early days.

CHANI: I had no idea that she had any feelings for me, because she didn't talk to me. She didn't acknowledge me most of the time. I was like, "All right, this woman—I don't know why she wants to do yoga with me. But she keeps showing up."

And so when she left LA—I think the distance helped you have courage. We had sessions online, and I was like, "Wait a minute, something's going on here." And I've never in my life ever experienced that—I do not date my clients. So I was like, "Look, I think there's chemistry here. I cannot be your yoga teacher."

SONYA: And all I heard was that she thought there was chemistry between us. So it was a victory from that point.

They spent their first six weeks dating from across the country—Sonya in New York and Chani in Los Angeles—with hours-long FaceTime calls (the "get-to-know-you" period, they've called it). Their first in-person date was a long weekend in New York. "We had three nights together, and when she left for the airport, my whole face was numb because my cheekbones were sore from laughing so much," Sonya told *Out* magazine years later.

Their relationship moved fast—it would take them only nine months to move in together in LA and get married. But they had one significant hurdle to get past. Until Sonya met Chani, she hadn't even been out to herself, let alone her very conservative family.

One of those nights in New York, she took Chani to a restaurant where everyone knew her and her family. It was supposed to be a loving gesture, inviting her into her world. "I remember, at the time," Sonya says, "I wouldn't hold her hand at the table."

SONYA: I wasn't actively trying to be in the closet—it was all very unconscious. So when we met, there was no internal resistance to falling in love with her. And there was no internal resistance to realizing I want to spend my life with her. It was really a couple months in where I was like, "Wait, does this mean I'm gay?"

It was like two o'clock in the morning, New York time; we were on FaceTime. And I was out loud, like, "Oh," and then a montage of my life is floating before my eyes. And I'm realizing how gay I am and how unaware of this I have been.

Chani was at a very different point in this journey when they met. She grew up in a small town in British Columbia "with an excellent amount of out queer people," she says. Her best friend's mom was a lesbian—her name was Casey; "super Dykes-on-Bikes kind of vibes"—and she was friends with Casey's girlfriend's daughter too. When Chani's dad got remarried, her stepmom's friends were all gay men. "I just had a roster of lesbians and gay men throughout my childhood."

By the time she met Sonya, Chani had been out "for like twenty years," she says. And going back into the closet wasn't an option for her. "I couldn't even if I wanted to," she said.

SONYA: Coming out to myself was not a difficult process at all. I didn't have shame—what I had was fear.

           We had a family friend. And he was friends with my brother, but we all played together. And I remember being eleven and coming downstairs to get a glass of water. Everyone in my family is huddled around in the kitchen, clearly having a very serious conversation. And I'm like, "What's going on?" And they were like, "We just found out so-and-so's gay." And I remember being like, "Obviously," and just walking up the stairs.

           And five minutes later, my mother burst into my room. I was punished so badly for knowing that this kid was gay and what that meant about me. It was one of the worst moments of my life.

She knew she couldn't think about coming out, she says, "until a point in my life where I could take care of myself. And that point in my life, extremely fortuitously, coincided with meeting the love of my life."

SONYA: At the time, I had been like, "Okay, I'm going to go home at Christmas and come out to my family." So we're talking like six months away. That was my plan. And when she said that [she couldn't go back into the closet], I did this very quick calculation in my head where I was like, "Oh, if I don't come out, if I don't do this part of my work, I'm going to lose this person that I want to spend the rest of my life with. So I've got to speed up my timeline." And a couple of weeks later, I came out to my family, and that was that. I just had to do the thing that was standing in the way of me being free.

Sonya doesn't want to get into how she left things with her family; she says, simply, "I got free. Let's put it that way." She dove into building this new world with Chani instead—and their personal and professional lives have been intertwined from the start.

SONYA: When we met seven years ago, Chani was not yet a full-time astrologer. But I remember reading her horoscopes and thinking she was just the most beautiful writer I had ever read. And she also had ten thousand followers on Facebook, which, seven years ago was like, "Wow, you're really popular." [author's note: She now runs more than half a million deep on social media.] And I remember thinking, "This person has so much untapped potential. And I know how to help." And so we started working together on Chani's business. Basically, within the first couple of weeks of meeting, I helped her set up things on her website. And then I started editing her horoscopes. But there was no intention in mind besides wanting to support her.

CHANI: I'm a typical Gen X. I grew up on my own, a total latchkey kid. I didn't know how to make dinner, basically. And she came along and she was like, "We eat three times a day, we plan things out, we budget," and I was like, "Whoa, this is so cool."

There's also an age gap between us—twelve years—so it's different generationally. And culturally—I grew up in Canada; she grew up in England. She has an Ivy League education; I grew up with a bunch of hippies that were like, "Whatever, man, it's cool." I didn't have any goals that were set up for me or even had myself. And she's all goals and strategy and finance spreadsheets.

Astrology, surprisingly, isn't a huge part of our conversation, but more than once, Chani points out that Sonya is an Aquarius. "Aquarius is logical," Chani says. "And she's such an Aquarius."

I think she's quick to point it out because it's the biggest difference between them: the strategist and the creative. And that difference is what's made them so successful as a unit—and, to borrow their word, part of what makes working together so exhilarating. With both of their hands on Chani's business, they have been able to grow it into something that can sustain them both. "I've always loved working on the business with Chani; I've always loved growing it," Sonya says. "The business became our foundation from which everything else grew."

SONYA: FreeFrom would not exist without Chani. Or at least it wouldn't have come as far as it did in the time that it has. Besides the fact that the business supported us so that I could be unpaid for two years and grow this thing, the first chunk of money we got was fundraising through your mailing list. And that chunk of money allowed me to hire my first staff member. FreeFrom has done phenomenal amounts of work in almost five years because we had that start.

OPPOSITE PAGE: Self-portrait, taken by Chani and Sonya.

All that said, Sonya didn't officially take a role in Chani Inc. until they started talking about building an app—a central, mobile location where people can find horoscopes, guided meditation, journaling prompts, and affirmations, all with the same progressive tone that Chani's work has always carried. They have an ongoing argument about whose idea that app was originally. "I'm convinced it's her idea, and she's convinced it was mine," Sonya says.

Chani shrugs. "I've never had such a good idea. So I just find it hard to think it was mine."

At that point, Chani asked Sonya to take over as CEO.

SONYA: The app hadn't been built yet. I was like, "Wait, are you saying you want me to be the one that builds it?" And she was like, "What did you think was happening around here? Where did you think this was going?"

CHANI: The thought that I would talk to a bunch of techies and tell them what to do? Well, this will never get built if you think that I'm going to do that with any success whatsoever. I literally, like, glaze over and start to pass out when people start talking code to me. I don't understand it. And it's easy for her. She just gets it.

SONYA: There was almost a new commitment to each other made, this time last year, where I was like, "Oh, I see. I really have to take a very purposeful role in the company now." Whereas before, I'd been supporting her with the things that she wanted to do. This now became really binding. It's like when we bought a house, and we were like, "Wow, if we got divorced, it's not easy anymore." And then when we launched the app, it was like, "Well, this just became even more binding and intricate and impossible to separate."

It's easy to miss in all of this that Sonya is also running a whole nonprofit. And a successful one, at that. FreeFrom's motivating principle is that the number one reason that domestic violence survivors stay in abusive situations is because they can't afford to leave—and no one should have to choose between abuse and homelessness. They provide a whole ecosystem of support to survivors, including emergency cash assistance, a savings matching program, and paid leave from work, all while advocating for policy changes on a state and federal level.

It's around this point in the explanation that I remember that she was, at one point, an investment banker. I ask her how she managed such a massive pivot from banking to domestic violence work. Both she and Chani are prepared for the question.

SONYA: Okay, this is the thing—

CHANI: The investment banking was the huge pivot.

SONYA: I've been doing domestic violence work since I was sixteen. I would run these Domestic Violence Awareness weeks at my high school where we'd raise money for local shelters. And then I went to college and started a group that was educating campus students and local high school students about intimate partner violence.

By this point, I knew that this was the work that I was going to do in the world—I had that very good fortune of figuring out at a young age what was my passion, what was my work. I decided to go to law school because I understood it to be a structural problem—it was presented to me within the context of human rights. So I decided I wanted to be a human rights lawyer.

CHANI: You would have been a great one.

SONYA: I don't know, it's not as . . .

CHANI: It's not as creative.

SONYA: But anyway, I decided to go to law school to give me an education on how you solve structural problems. And so my whole personal statement for law school was about ending violence against women. And I chose to go to Berkeley Law because they had such a strong domestic violence practice. And in my second year of law school, I actually started my first nonprofit, which is based in Oakland and still very much active and thriving and is creating good case law in California to support survivors through the courts.

So all of a sudden, in my second year of law school, this became my day job and being in law school became my night job. So I got very comfortable having two jobs very early in my life. And I loved it. I loved the process of starting it. I loved the process of galvanizing people around it. I loved the fundraising. I loved the strategy. And it really helped me to realize two things: how many gaps there were in our solution to the problem of intimate partner violence and that the part I wanted to play was filling those gaps.

CHANI: So when we first met, I was like, "Who is this person?" She's a banker. And then I went on her Facebook page and I saw all the stuff about that first org, and I was like, "Wait, she's really into that. She's really into working in this field."

And I was like, "Wow, that's amazing." Because I was really looking for a relationship at that point. And I wasn't into dating anybody that wasn't at least trying to fulfill their life purpose in some way, shape, or form. And so when I saw that, I was like, "Oh, she's really serious."

That became especially clear on one of their phone dates when they were still living in different states.

CHANI: We were on the phone, and she was like, "Oh, can you just hold on a second? Right now [my org] is running a fundraiser." Now I was like, "Oh, what's going on?" She's like, "Oh, well, they're doing a battle of the bands right now." I was like, "This second?" She was like, "Yeah, just give me two secs." And she came back. And I was like, "How much are you raising?" And she was like, "Two hundred and fifty thousand dollars." "You're casually raising two hundred and fifty thousand dollars on the phone with me right now."

SONYA: Listen, I might not have been out of the closet, but . . .

CHANI: She was able to do this huge thing. And then investment banking is a very involved thing. If you work in that field, you're on call all the time, you're texting with people all the time, you're emailing people at three in the morning. And she had this way of being able to do like these two jobs at the same time and then give me all of her attention. She's an incredibly intense person.

SONYA: Incredibly.

CHANI: It was very impressive. I've never met anybody who could just, you know, raise $250,000 in a second.

SONYA: I have significant gray hairs for a thirty-three-year-old.

CHANI: I was like, "Wait, how are you an activist and you're in this horrible thing like investment banking?" And she was like, "Well, this is how I'm gonna get the money and funnel it to the things that I want to funnel it to." And I was like, "All right, I just don't see that for you."

Earlier, Sonya had talked about how little shame she had around being gay. She was afraid to tell her family for practical reasons, not because of shame she held herself. But in her anti-violence work—the work she was most passionate about, the work that was closest to her heart—she held a kind of shame that had echoes of being closeted.

SONYA: It wasn't my shame; it was family shame—this idea that that work wasn't the work to do. I should be a doctor or a lawyer or a banker. And when I started my first organization, I didn't tell my family for like a year because I just knew it wasn't going to go well.

I had strategic reasons for doing banking. I learned in starting my first organization that if you're running a nonprofit, you're running a business, and people fail when they forget that they're running a business. You need to know accounting, and you need to know money. Everyone thinks you're just some savior doing the Lord's work, and so you don't have to have any firm understanding of the structure of it. And I realized that was not true.

And then the other reason is, I was sort of giving into my family's desire for me. I had made peace in my mind that I would continue to be involved in anti-violence work my whole life, but I wasn't allowed to do it. And at that point in my life, I was still in the family system enough to really believe that I wasn't allowed to do it. And when Chani and I met, the first gift she gave me was helping me realize that there was nothing to be ashamed of. And that this really was my work. And this really was my calling. And honestly, it didn't take that long to strip away that shame, as long as I could logically understand what's going on.

CHANI: She's such an Aquarius.

I ask them if they ever try to create boundaries between their work life and their relationship. And true to Sonya, they have systems. On Fridays, starting at noon, they go to a restaurant or a café and have a six- or seven-hour business meeting—channeling all the thoughts, problems, obstacles that come up in their business throughout the week instead of doing this in the kitchen or when they're trying to wind down on the couch. "We had to set rules for this," Sonya says. "Once we start brushing our teeth for bed, there's no talking about work."

CHANI: And we break them all the time.

SONYA: All the time.

CHANI: The other one will be like, "You can't talk about work now. We talk about this on Monday. You schedule a meeting with me. Can you write this down?"

SONYA: We do our very best. This is the first year of our relationship where we don't work evenings and weekends. And that's huge for us to have time where we're just enjoying each other.

CHANI: We're good at turning off when we turn off. And we've had to create those boundaries. And in the beginning, there was just so much potential and so much work we had to get done that we worked nonstop for like six years. I remember when we first got together, we were in New York. And it was like, I don't know, probably at ten o'clock at night, I was, like, writing, working. And I looked over at her and she was working. And I just got the sense like, "Whoa, she works as hard as me and harder." And that was both thrilling and then, I think, deeply exhausting. We're, both of us, just really intense people. And I think we've also poured a lot of our life's energy into our work.

At the end of our conversation, I realize that we've spent almost all of our time talking about their work. But when I listen to it again, I realize it was by design—talking about their work was, in a lot of ways, the same as talking about their relationship.

And that made one part of the interview feel especially poignant. One of the questions we asked every couple in this book was "What do you love about your partner's work?"

For Chani, Sonya's work with FreeFrom feeds a part of her that she can't nurture on her own.

CHANI: It was always really important that I end up with somebody that was an activist, because I think, at heart, that's what I'm interested in. It's just that my skills are more like helping other people personally connect with what it is they're supposed to do in the world. The part of me that wants to externalize that and be a part of changing and creating the world that you want—I realized that I probably wasn't going to do that work specifically, so I wanted that to be present in the relationship.

FreeFrom is changing the landscape of how the gender-based-violence movement does its work. It's innovating upon decades of other people's work in a long lineage of working to relieve the systemic ways in which intimate partner violence exists and how it exists

TOP IMAGE: Chani, photographed by Sonya.

LEFT IMAGE: Sonya, photgraphed by Chani.

and why it exists and how it thrives, why it thrives, and what to do very clearly, succinctly, and strategically to interrupt it. It's such elegant work—the ways in which FreeFrom approaches the problem is clear, it's precise, it's thoughtful, it's mindful, it's compassionate, it's full of care.

There's so many issues in the world. And I think it's really, for me, find something you're passionate about, focus on it, and put your talent there; and through that, other things will also get healed, or other people can do the other pieces of the work.

I've been impacted by intimate partner violence. I grew up in so much of it, it was just everywhere, almost every single relationship in one way or another in my childhood had it. I grew up in a town just full of it. So it helps to heal my own trauma around that. It helps to heal my own loneliness, knowing that people are finding meaning and purpose and healing and a pathway to something that is about them understanding their own agency. To address that—to be like, "This is how we can fuck with the system. Let's bust it open"—is really exhilarating.

SONYA: My spokesperson.

What do I love about her work? Everything. It's exhilarating to work with her. She is my favorite writer. And she is my favorite communicator, and I love all the different ways that she now communicates her message. She's a brilliant teacher, she's a healer—she helped me start healing real quick after we met. And she just has so much integrity in everything that she does.

What she's doing at the core of everything is supporting people in living their best lives, living out their purpose, and that can sound really gimmicky and self-help-y, but she did it for me. My life is completely different because she helped me accept and love what I'm here to do.

So I always say to people, if we can all just make peace with and undo the shame of what our real talent is, what our real gifts are, we can contribute so much to the world, we can create so much healing for ourselves and our communities and everyone else. And she approaches astrology—which is, you know, ancient—but she approaches it with this goal and this mission, and to me, if we do nothing else with our lives, if we can help people see that they have this map of what they're bringing into the world and what they can do with it—there's no greater gift you can give someone.

They take so much pride in what they've created. When we talked in 2021, their work seemed, in some ways, like their family.

SONYA: Everything that we've created is—as cheesy as it sounds—our love and our commitment to each other kind of externalized. We're most driven to create. It's what we're doing in this life.

Two years later, we reached out to confirm a few details about how their work and life were balanced— the "No Work After Toothbrushing" rule, the Friday business meeting. But none of that is the same, they told us. Because they're now the parents of a six-month-old child.

They're still running both companies—this was the same year that Chani Inc. was singled out by Forbes for proving that you could pay your staff fairly, have a four-day workweek, and still grow by half every year. But "becoming parents has completely reoriented our lives and our worlds," they told us.

"It's deepened our commitment to the ways in which we are a team," they said—a new dimension to the partnership they've been cultivating for a decade. "We are still coming to terms with all the ways in which these shifts manifest, but one thing is for sure—it's the most fun we've ever had."

ANDRIA WILSON MIRZA

(SHE/HER)
DIRECTOR OF REFRAME

FAWZIA MIRZA

(SHE/THEY)
FILMMAKER

MIRACULOUSLY, AS FAR AS WE KNOW, no one in these pages has an ex in this book. But over the two years that we were meeting and interviewing couples, it became clearer and clearer just how interconnected our queer circles can be. Most of them are barely one-degree separated from another couple in here: When we were in LA, we found out that three couples in this book were in the same regular lesbian poker game; we'd show up at photo shoots and find out that another couple had already told them how their own shoot had gone. Some people nominated couples they thought should be in the book; others lit up when they found out their friends were already in it.

But nothing beats Fawzia and Andria. "Chani married us!" they both announced when we first met.

The couple has known Chani and Sonya as long as they've been together. Chani and Sonya have been enthusiastic supporters of their work: The year we met both couples, Fawzia's thirteen-minute short *Noor & Layla* had just been released—a queer, Muslim film in five acts, one for each time of prayer. Chani and Sonya were both executive producers.

But perhaps more importantly, Andria and Fawzia credit both Chani and Sonya with getting them down the aisle: "Both the act—Sonya was our witness and Chani was our officiant," Fawzia says, but also "the greater kind of spiritual reason."

The way Fawzia tells it, she and Andria had been dating for a while, and she knew without a doubt that she was in love with her. "Sonya has this incredible, wise, elder quality to her. And when she cares, it's deep," Fawzia says.

So she asked Fawzia: "Okay, then, what are your intentions?"

Today, Fawzia acknowledges that she was dealing with an intense fear of commitment. She'd been out for years at that point, but she comes from a very conservative Muslim and Pakistani family. "There has been a history of what I thought love and romance was supposed to look like," she says, "growing up Pakistani and watching Bollywood films of great love and romance. And what a wedding is supposed to look like—how your family is supposed to be there and they're supposed to give you jewelry and feed you sweets."

But at the time, her response to Sonya was: "Yeah, but . . . maybe I'm poly!"

FAWZIA: The closer we got, Sonya started to analyze and dig into what that really was about. Both of them being so connected to the sky—knowing my astrology, I am deeply monogamous, both in my chart and in my patterns of life.
             So when she dug a little deeper and asked, "Well, why do you think that you might want to be with other people?" And I said, "Well, I actually don't want to be with

anybody else. But what if in five years I meet someone that I'm supposed to be with, or what if something happens and I become a different person?"

Sonya listened patiently. And when Fawzia was done, she reminded her: "You're literally living for something that may never happen."

FAWZIA: And it was a moment of great reflection for me—like the boulder was lifted and I was able to get out of my own way.

And suddenly it just was like, "Oh yeah, we're just in love." And that means we can do whatever we want.

"And a great day was coming up," Fawzia says, "02/02/2020, a perfect palindrome." (This was the second couple we talked to who had strong feelings about their wedding date: Before Covid hit, Roxane and Debbie were supposed to get married on 10/10/20. Roxane still isn't over it.) Chani agreed to officiate and confirmed that it was a good astrology day—and that the best time for their ceremony would be between eleven thirty and twelve.

FAWZIA: And I feel like Venus—I'm ruled deeply by Venus—Venus was doing the best things.

ANDRIA: The best things.

FAWZIA: Venus was doing her dance, you know?

ANDRIA: I had been at Sundance, and I remember being on the phone with Fawz and, like, "Are we—should we—we'll just do it, then. Yeah, we'll just do it." And then basically went into mini-event-production mode.

I went and got a haircut, and at the store right next to where I was getting my hair cut, I saw this dress and I was like, "That seems good." And the same day, got on the plane. And I flew on the red-eye, and then the next morning, we woke up here in LA and we went and got our license.

FAWZIA: We had samosas and mimosas because that felt appropriate. And a friend of ours was living on this small urban farm in Laurel Canyon with a couple goats and chickens and things. We invited like fifteen people—none of my blood family was there; it was just Andria and some of our LA community—close friends and collaborators, and literally the week before, it came together.

After the party, as the day wound down, they got into a cab, headed to LAX, and boarded a flight. They spent their wedding night on a red-eye to Toronto.

"It was pretty fitting," Andria says. That's because when they got married, Andria and Fawzia had never lived in the same country together.

They tell me this story from their home in LA—a relatively new phenomenon, and one they're clearly still getting used to. By the time we meet up with them in 2021, Andria is the director of ReFrame, the gender equity initiative of the Sundance Institute, and Fawzia has just finished directing her third film since lockdown started.

But when they met in 2017, Andria was the executive director of a Canadian LGBTQ film festival called Inside Out in Toronto, and Fawzia was living in Chicago and had written and starred in her first feature film, *Signature Move* (the tagline was "Life, love, and lady wrestling").

ANDRIA: We programmed it at Inside Out as our big women's gala film. And so we met at the festival and learned when we met in person that we both had actually grown up in the same very tiny part of Canada—

FAWZIA: In Nova Scotia—sort of like Canadian Maine. Lots of lobsters, the Atlantic Ocean, that whole thing. And cold. Don't stand by the ocean in the winter.

We definitely had a very instant connection and chemistry. I was in a relationship at the time. Andria—this was her first year at the festival, in this whole new big job. I'd screened some of my work at the festival before, but as is film festival life, you just start to see and meet each other in other cities over and over and over again. That was the year that I traveled to all sorts of places. I went to India right before I met her, with the film. I was in Greece, I was in the UK, and it was just a lot of traveling, and we would have this group of friends that we kept seeing on the circuit.

I moved to LA in 2018 to write for a TV show that summer. And when Andria came for Outfest in July, I was out of my relationship, and we really started dating. And have never stopped.

ANDRIA: Still dating.

FAWZIA: Still dating.

Fawzia was firmly based in LA by then, but as the director of a film festival, a huge part of Andria's job was traveling from festival to festival all around the world. Plus, she didn't have a visa to work in the United States.

So they'd find a weekend here, a weekend there, and they built their relationship on a foundation of hotel stays and rides to the airport.

FAWZIA: She's the person who would take the red-eye and come visit me on a Friday after work from Toronto to LA, stay till Sunday, take the red-eye, go straight to work, and be the boss who ran the organization and was just able to do that.

ANDRIA: Well, honestly, it just made sense. This was what our relationship could be, and it was never a difficult choice for me. I would just look at the calendar and see those two days and be like, "That's the longest time period I have. So I want to spend it with Fawzia." And it just meant that in the time that we were together, we were fully together, you know?

Long distance may not be the path for everyone. But we were fully formed adults when we got into this relationship; we're not twenty-five. And it was a really good way for us to build our relationship—because we had these fully formed, very busy separate lives. And so to be able to have the committed time together, when we had it, was really beautiful. And then to be able to continue to grow our own individual lives and careers at the same time was what we both needed.

There wasn't necessarily an end in sight either when they flew to Toronto the day they got married. Andria was still running a Canadian festival—and still didn't have a work visa in the US—and Fawzia was still firmly based in LA. But their wedding was on 02/02/2020—a month before Covid lockdowns started.

FAWZIA: So we made the decision that I'm not going back in case the borders closed. We just got married; we're going to stay together. So I had, truly, just a carry-on suitcase, and I lived in Toronto for a year with my tiny suitcase.

ANDRIA: We were in Toronto for the full pandemic, and then Fawz came back here to LA to shoot a film in February of '21. And at that time I had accepted a new job that is here in LA, but they were working on my work visa, which, due to Covid, everything was, like, taking so long. So I didn't actually get here until April.

At this point, Fawzia starts stumbling over her words *a lot*.

FAWZIA: By the way, she just glossed over like the additional trau—I mean, not that I mean, and not to go—Yeah, I mean that's, that's it, say that, but, yeah, she, we went, yeah—

ANDRIA: Was that a sentence?

FAWZIA: She glossed over one of the biggest things that happened!

Truly one of the most life-changing things that happened to us during Covid was Andria was diagnosed with cervical cancer. We were going to come back to LA in October, but then we got this diagnosis, and it was like, "We need to stay in Canada." And one month led to another to another—as you know the system is wonderful there, and it also is a different kind of system where you're just sort of waiting for the parts to move. So she had surgery. She's, thank God, healthy, and they got everything. And she's doing really, really well.

But that was a really additionally life-changing moment. Seeing someone you love just completely debilitated, not able to walk. And I was just like, "Oh, my whole life was about all of these other parts falling in place so that I could care for her."

ANDRIA: Because if it wasn't for the pandemic, we wouldn't have been living together. It wasn't in our plan necessarily to be living together full-time until I was able to work in the US. So it was only because of the pandemic that Fawz was in Canada. It was because of the pandemic that I was in Canada longer than expected and got my diagnosis in Canada and got to be cared for by the Canadian health-care system and come through it so successfully. So how do we even process that we feel so lucky and all of this happened because of this seismic global event and tragedy?

But because of lockdown, protocols in the hospitals were extremely strict in Canada. "So through the entire medical process, I wasn't able to have Fawzia with me at all," Andria says, "even though we were legally married."

ANDRIA: One of the great things about our relationship and our partnership is that I'm someone who never asked for help ever in my life. And Fawzia will ask anyone for help and also offer help to everyone. She's just always in that space of giving love and also accepting love and support from others.

And so, in the health-care system—

FAWZIA: —you have to have someone to advocate—

ANDRIA: —advocate for you. And so I knew that if I had been able to have her with me in person, it would have definitely made a huge difference.

They both talk about the experience as radicalizing. "Gynecological health is an incredibly difficult space to navigate as a queer person," Andria says. "As a queer woman, those spaces can be intimidating because you have to come out to everyone through every step of the process."

It gave them a new perspective on the importance of consistent access to care. The cancer Andria had progresses on a schedule, "and getting a pap saved her life," says Fawzia. "Another six months of not having that test, the cancer could have spread much further."

Andria's cancer defined one huge contour in their Covid lockdown era. But it was also the first time that they were able to share the kind of passive intimacy that comes with living day-to-day with your partner. And that was a huge inspiration for Fawzia. *Noor & Layla*, the short that Chani and Sonya produced, was "inspired by moments I shared with [Andria] sheltering in place in Toronto during the month of Ramadan in 2020," she told the *Advocate*. "During that time, we shared many rituals together, Ramadan rituals and also marriage rituals that we didn't get to have at our wedding. It reminded me [of] the importance of celebrating our love and triumphs in ways that matter to us."

FAWZIA: In the film, there's a scene where the two queer women put henna on each other. There's this story in South Asian wedding culture that when you get henna, if you put the name of the person you're marrying in their hand somewhere, you hide it, and then the other person has to find it. Those rituals weren't a part of our wedding ceremony, and so we got henna [during lockdown], and we're just writing each other's names on each other's bodies with it.

Celebrating our love outside of the system that won't accept us—it took me my whole life to get there. And I still don't have the acceptance of a lot of the Muslim community, or many blood relatives, nor does Andria. And yet we are thriving. And some of that is through that chosen family who walks with us and who celebrates us when those others don't, and some of that is the art that we can create and have that space to show other people that love like that love is possible. It is happening. And you are fucking beautiful, and you deserve it.

With all that in mind, when I asked them where they might want to do their photo shoot for this book, I expected that they'd want to capture the home they've built together now that they're finally able to live in the same place. And they thought about it for a couple weeks, but ultimately, they decided that a hotel room was truest to them. "We grew our relationship by meeting in other cities," Fawzia says. So their relationship was built in hotels and cabs and airports (that was also on the table, but we couldn't figure out how to work around TSA).

When I asked if a hotel room would feel like an artifact in their life now that they live together—a part of their history rather than the world they're living in now—they were very quick to correct me.

Andria, photographed by Fawzia.

When one of them is on a deadline or needs a change of space for a creative project, their first move is to get a hotel room.

And it seems if one of them is on deadline, the other one probably is too. "I feel like we work on literally everything together," Andria says. "All the time." So I ask if they have a favorite thing they've created together. At first, Fawzia mentions *Noor & Layla*, but then she stops herself.

FAWZIA: There's two answers. Building a life is the greatest collaboration. Because it just feels like things make sense now. So now we can build together.

And part of why Chani and Sonya are so important in our lives is we need role models. We need to see people around ourselves that are great examples of the thing that we want to be. And as queer people, you don't always have that. Being around them, I saw like, "Oh, that's what I want." And that is inspiring to me and to us as we move day-to-day, trusting that there is something bigger for us, building.

I feel like every project we do together is just an affirmation that we were right—to be together and work together. And it then becomes another component of our relationship that we're building on. And when we made this short film *Noor & Layla* in Toronto during the pandemic, it was a really beautiful expression of so many things that we want to do with our work. We wanted to show queer love and a multifaceted queer relationship. And bring together a team who also had those values and was also passionate about authentic representation and was also bringing their lived experiences to the work.

All of Fawzia's work explores how queerness interacts with other parts of our identities—race, religion, family. But they balance on this razor edge of telling those stories without boiling people down into their categories. By all critical accounts, she's quite successful.

FAWZIA: We had this tiny, tiny budget project, but everyone who was on set, everyone who was a part of the process was very much in that space. So it was an opportunity for us to really put the challenge to ourselves: "Can we not just have these values but live these values together?" And that was an affirmation that we can do that.

And so now, with each subsequent project and working toward this feature that we're going to shoot next year, it's all about "How do we hold on to that truth and what we want to accomplish together and not lose that in the machine of Hollywood?" And one of the goals is decolonizing storytelling and decolonizing the set and not bringing those things into our relationship because they just don't serve.

Fawzia, photographed by Andria.

One by-product of exploring identity in her work as much as she does, though, is that audiences want to know whose voice they're hearing, so she finds herself talking about their own relationship to those identities a lot. When we speak, she has just come off three different panels, and she told her coming-out story at every one. ("Andria says it's like therapy.")

FAWZIA: I came out at the age of twenty-nine. But it was such a process. So it took a few years—three, four years.

When I think about the phrase *coming out*—this is something that I have reflected on a lot and I didn't have the language at the time—but coming out is such a white, Western term.

Growing up conservative Muslim, South Asian, I wasn't allowed to date or drink or wear shorts or eat pork and couldn't go to prom or date boys. So what was I going to tell my mom? Like, "Mom, I'm suddenly having sex with women"? We didn't even use the word *sex*. So what was I going to come out about?

So that process was much more complicated and layered for me and my family. And my first girlfriend I lived with—I told my mom I had a roommate for three years. Needless to say, it was a tough breakup.

Then, when I moved out, I told my mom that she wasn't my roommate, she was my girlfriend. If you told me ten, fifteen years ago that I'd be talking to my mom about my wife, and my mom wouldn't be mad about it all the time, I'd be shocked. So the fact that we've gotten to this place is pretty great.

When Andria starts to share her relationship with her family, she dips her toe in slowly. "They're still based in Canada, but not in my life day-to-day," she says. "It's a mutual situation."

Fawzia quickly jumps in: "But they're homophobic."

Andria's family is conservative and very Christian, and queerness was simply "not an option," she says.

ANDRIA: I was definitely bred for marriage. I was dating women when I was a teenager and left home—as a teenager—because of it, and then spent the next few years trying to get back into my family's good graces. Eventually, after lots of work and therapy, I figured out that I was chasing something that didn't serve me, or them, and certainly not the people that I was in relationships with.

A lot of us come from conservative backgrounds. And that's not specific just to one religion. I remember us having a conversation with someone who assumed that—because Fawzia comes from a Muslim family and I come from a conservative Christian family—I would have a relationship with my parents and she would not. And, I mean, that's Islamophobic. But also, there's so many different kinds of conservativism. And there's also so many people that have kids and don't necessarily have the tools to nurture them. And that's real too.

I don't think I really came out publicly till my late twenties because when I was working as an actor, I was very clearly told by my agents and people I was working with that I would never be successful if I did. What I really understand to be true now—everyone was telling me that the men who run this industry need to believe that they can have sex with you or you will not be successful—and that is rape culture. And so in the work that we do now, that continues to be a source of inspiration—showing folks that, literally, you can have any job and bring your authentic self to that.

That notion seems to play a role in everything they do. As the director of ReFrame, Andria's job is specifically to undermine biases in hiring in the film industry, from the cast to the crew.

And Fawzia is consistently creating, directing, and shaping the characters they never had when they were growing up. When I ask them both if they remember the first person they recognized as queer, Fawz gets really excited at first. ("Real or on a show? Anything? Oh, my God, it's such a good question.") But she quickly realizes she can't come up with something. "I don't know my answer," she says, turning to Andria. "What do you think my answer is?"

FAWZIA: I know that when I was a kid, there's a boy that I grew up with who was also South Asian and Muslim and was raised the same. And I didn't really understand what it meant, but people were like, "Oh, he's different." And there was definitely coded language.

There were definitely people in between this, but I remember there was an uncle. We called him an uncle when I was living in Chicago. And he's a famous poet who's since passed. His name was Ifti Nasim, and I was working on some project—I hadn't made my own work yet. But I was helping on some other projects. And I was in the South Asian community, on my own, not with my parents in Chicago, and was connected to a couple men and one of them was this poet. And I remember one of the other men after the poet left, and he said, "How do you like him? He's colorful, huh?" And this was, you know, a South Asian man referring to another South Asian man. And I was like, "What is he saying?" And I had started dating my—I was with my first girlfriend at the time, but I still was trying to understand what *gay* was in my own community.

ANDRIA: I think that in the medium that we work in, the conversation has very recently started to shift just from onscreen representation to actual narrative sovereignty and liberation, and not just diversity but inclusion and belonging. All these conversations are really just kind of starting to find their footing. And that very much affects me and how I think about our own responsibility in communicating what it means to be a queer person or person of all of these identities in the world and in the work.

If we only see one kind of queer person thriving, that limits us in the same way that if we only see one particular portrayal of trans people, that's going to impact us or make us feel like we're growing up kind of invisible, right? Because I've never seen someone like me in media. So I think in this current space, it's deeper than just the surface level of representation. It's also like, how are we bringing that, like, full authentic self and narrative to the world?

FAWZIA: Growing up South Asian, on TV there was Mindy Kaling and Apu on *The Simpsons*. That was the South Asian representation. And with Apu, you're like, "Well, he's animated. Also, am I supposed to *be* Apu? Or marry Apu? How am I supposed to be a gay brown woman? How does this make sense?" There was nowhere to go up. There was nowhere to look.

And whether I knew I was doing it or not, at some point I made it my mission to be out and to love. And that was always my dream, because I knew if I was really out there, and really not lying to myself, I knew it also was a reflection of self-love. Our capacity to love another is a great reflection of the healing that we've done within.

Regardless of what I'm doing, I get messages from people all the time that are like, "I never saw a queer Muslim person until you," and I was like, "I didn't either!" and now I have this community of people that inspires me, and that's what keeps me going.

In that spirit, they both seem very aware that their relationship itself—outside of their professional lives—contributes to the queer canon of visibility. They hold that responsibility with the weight it deserves—like their marriage is a project that they need to build and grow. "We got married officially in 2020," Fawzia says. "But we've made it a commitment that every year we will recommit to each other. Because we don't want this to be something that fizzles and fades and dies—of course it will evolve and shift and change, but we want our commitment to evolve and shift and change with it."

For their first anniversary, on 02/02/2021, they had a nikah, an Islamic marriage ceremony, performed by a queer brown imam. "And in the Muslim commitment ceremony, there is kind of an exchange that's supposed to happen. We're coming from these old rituals of 'What are you giving? Is there land? Is there money in exchange? A contract?' What we exchanged was a promise. And the promise was 'I promise to love myself first so I can love you better.'"

"I take it really personally—in a good way—when folks reflect how much they love us as a couple," Fawzia says. "Getting to this point of being able to love Andria so fully and completely. To me, that's been my life's work."

AFTERWORD

I STILL THINK IT'S WILD that this is going to be a book. On shelves. In libraries. Maybe on someone's bedside or coffee table. Billie and I both come from the magazine world, so our lives have been defined by news pegs and issues that always end up in the recycling, eventually.

But this project—with a spine that shouts "queer power"—takes up space. Physical space. It takes up space with queer love and excellence.

And perhaps most importantly, it takes up space with queer joy.

I said in the Intro that if you take away anything from this book, I hope it's queer joy. A lot of people in this book only grew up with examples of queer pain or trauma or struggle—TV characters dying of AIDS, family members ostracized when they came out. While I was working on this book, I published almost a dozen news stories that cataloged the harm we've experienced: the wave of trans medical care bans, the Trump administration's erosion of LGBTQ protections, and the threat to marriage equality when abortion protections were overturned.

And it is important for people in power to hear about our pain. But it too often becomes what defines us. In her book *The Tragedy of Heterosexuality*, Jane Ward suggests that we "consider that one of the ways heteronormativity sustains itself is by telling and retelling a story about how heterosexuality makes people happy, while queerness produces difficulty and suffering. This story about queer suffering under the force of heteronormativity is true; but it is also only a sliver of the story about queerness, and it is one that masks not only queer joy and pleasure, but also queer relief not to be straight."

In these pages, there are stories of rejection and loss and confusion, but every single story is also a queer love story. Every single story shows access to queer joy and queer fulfillment and queer success. And we deserve to see all of it.

Barbara Belmont and Shelley Diamond.

"The pain is still always a part of it. It's a very messy process. And it can be a very ugly process," ND Stevenson told us. "But being queer has only brought me joy, and everything about this is making my life bigger and making me more capable of joy."

I thought about my eight-year-old self a lot while we worked on this project—watching Spinelli and wondering what it was we had in common. Making this book—a compendium of queer representation—feels like a gift we wish we could go back in time and give to our younger selves: to hand it to them and say, "See? Your future is full of possibility."

We hope this book offers a few more maps, torches, and possible selves: a catalog of trails that have already been carved out by queer people who are changing the world in their own way, not in spite of their queerness, but at least, in part, because of it.

MAKING THIS BOOK
HAS GIVEN US
IMMENSE QUEER
JOY. WE HOPE
READING IT DID
THE SAME FOR YOU.

HANNAH MURPHY WINTER

(SHE/THEY)

is a journalist who writes about queerness and policies that impact LGBTQ+ lives. Her work frequently appears in *Rolling Stone*. She lives in Seattle with her wife, Billie Winter, three cats they found in their shed, and their rescue dog, Pippin. The first person she ever recognized as queer was Spinelli from *Recess*.

BILLIE WINTER

(SHE/HER)

is a photographer and videographer. She grew up in Queens, NY, and worked at *Rolling Stone* as a photo editor for fifteen years until she moved to Seattle and became an organic, regenerative farmer. She still has a crush on Cheetara from *Thundercats*.